Kipling's Pocket History of England

Kipling's Pocket History of England

BY
C. R. L. FLETCHER
AND
RUDYARD KIPLING

Pictures by Henry Ford

Greenwich House
Distributed by Crown Publishers, Inc.
New York

This 1983 edition is published by Greenwich House,
a division of Arlington House, Inc.,
distributed by Crown Publishers, Inc., by arrangement with
Doubleday & Company, Inc.

Manufactured in the United States of America

Library of Congress Cataloging in Publication Data

Fletcher, C. R. L. (Charles Robert Leslie), 1857-1934.
  Kipling's pocket history of England.

  Reprint. Originally published: A history of England.
Garden City, N.Y.: Doubleday, Page, 1911.
  1. Great Britain—History.   I. Kipling, Rudyard,
1865-1936.   II. Title.
DA32.F66   1983   941   82-18366

ISBN: 0-517-402459

h g f e d c b a

PREFACE

THIS book is written for all boys and girls who are interested in the story of Great Britain and her Empire.

C. R. L. F.
R. K.

March, 1911.

THE original publishers desire to express their thanks to the Manager and officials of the United Services Museum, Whitehall, for their courtesy in giving facilities to the artist for making studies of the military and naval material in the museum.

CONTENTS

POEMS

LIST OF DRAWINGS

LIST OF MAPS

CHAPTER I

FROM THE EARLIEST TIME TO THE DEPARTURE OF THE ROMANS

The River's Tale

Twenty bridges from Tower to Kew
Wanted to know what the River knew,
For they were young and the Thames
* was old,*
And this is the tale that the River told:

I walk my beat before London Town,
Five hours up and seven down.
Up I go and I end my run
At Tide-end-town, which is Teddington.
Down I come with the mud in my hands
And plaster it over the Maplin Sands.
But I'd have you know that these waters
    of mine
Were once a branch of the River Rhine,
When hundreds of miles to the east I went
And England was joined to the Continent.

I remember the bat-winged lizard-birds,
The Age of Ice and the mammoth herds,
And the giant tigers that stalked them
    down
Through Regent's Park into Camden Town.
And I remember like yesterday
The earliest Cockney who came my way
When he pushed through the forest that
    lined the Strand,
With paint on his face and a club in his
    hand.
He was death to feather and fin and fur,
He trapped my beavers at Westminster,
He netted my salmon, he hunted my
    deer,
He killed my herons off Lambeth Pier;
He fought his neighbour with axes and
    swords,
Flint or bronze, at my upper fords.

While down at Greenwich for slaves and
    tin
The tall Phœnician ships stole in,
And North Sea war-boats, painted and
    gay,
Flashed like dragon-flies Erith way;
And Norseman and Negro and Gaul
    and Greek.
Drank with the Britons in Barking Creek,

And life was gay, and the world was new,
And I was a mile across at Kew!
But the Roman came with a heavy hand,
And bridged and roaded and ruled the land,
And the Roman left and the Danes blew
    in —
And that's where your history books
    begin!

THIS is to be a short history of all the people
who have lived in the British Islands. I have
just counted up over a hundred of these islands
on the map, some of them mere rocks, some as
big as small counties; besides England with
Scotland, and Ireland. But when first there
were men in Britain it was not a group of islands, but one stretch of land joining the great
continent of Europe, which then reached out
into the Atlantic Ocean more than fifty miles
west of Ireland. The English Channel, the
North Sea, and the Irish Sea were then land
through which ran huge European rivers.
The land was covered with forests and swamps
and full of wild beasts, some of which have now
vanished from the earth, while others, such
as the tiger and the elephant, have gone to
warmer climates. As for wolves, the land was
alive with them. Indeed, the last wolf in
Scotland was killed only 240 years ago; the

last in Ireland about 180 years ago. The beaver was one of the commonest animals of those early times, and perhaps helped to make our flat meadows by the dams he built across the streams.

But we know almost nothing about the first men who lived here, except that they were Perhaps 50,000 years ago. The first men. naked and very hairy; they slept in trees and lived on raw flesh or fruit, or dug for roots with crooked branches. After a long while, probably thousands of years, the climate got gradually colder, and great sheets of ice covered all Northern Europe. Then these first men either died out or went away southward. Again thousands of years passed, and the west end of Europe got freed of ice and sank several hundred feet, and the sea flooded over the lower parts. So Britain became an island or a group of islands.

Perhaps 10,000 years ago. The Cave men. Then the second race of men came, perhaps in some kind of boats made of skins stretched over bent poles. About this race we do know something. They were jolly, cunning, dark little fellows with long black hair. At first they lived high up on the hills, so that they could see their enemies from a distance. They could cook food, they dug out caves to live in, they made arrows and axes of sharp stones, and so stood a very fair chance of fighting the wild beasts. Their brains, though perhaps small compared to ours, were worth all the strength of all the beasts that ever howled at night. No doubt they had still something of the beast in them; they could run very swiftly; could climb trees like monkeys; could smell their enemies and their prey far off. They grew up early and died young. Most of their children died in infancy. They clothed themselves in skins, and at first lived entirely by hunting and fishing. Their whole time was devoted to getting food for themselves and their families. But just think what a lot of things they had to make for themselves. How long it must have taken to polish a piece of flint until it was sharp enough to cut down a tree or to cut up a tough old wolf! How long to make a fish-hook or a needle of bone! How clever and hard-working these men must have been! No doubt there were a few sneaks and lazy wretches then, as there are now, who tried to beg from other people instead of fighting for themselves and their wives. But I fancy such fellows had a worse time of it then than they have now. A man who wouldn't work very soon died.

Life of the Cave men.

No doubt there were holidays, too, after a successful hunt; or long lazy summer days, when it was too hot to go out after deer or

bison, and when even the women laid aside
their everlasting skin-stitching and told each
other stories of their babies; and the babies
toddled about after butterflies, larger and
brighter than the peacocks and tortoise shells
of to-day. I don't suppose that these men
thought of Britain as their "country"; but
they thought of their family or their tribe as
something sacred, for which they would fight
and die; and the spirit of the good land took
hold of them, the smell of the good damp mother-
earth, the hum of the wild bees, the rustle of
Their animals. heather and murmur of fern; they made rude
songs about it, and carved pictures of their
fights on the shoulder-blades of the beasts
they had killed. As time went on they grew
still more cunning, and began to tame the
young of some of the beasts, such as puppies,
lambs, calves and kids; and they found out
the delights of a good drink of milk. And
Corn growing. so to the hunting trade they added the shepherd's trade, which is a much more paying one.
Then some wonderful fellow discovered how
to sow seeds of wheat, or some other corn;
and that these, when ripened, gathered and
ground to powder, made a delicious food, which
we call bread. When that was found out real
civilization began; for a third trade was added,
that of agriculture, the most paying of all.

So one by one the earth gave up her secrets to our forefathers, and, like Adam and Eve, they went forth to subdue and replenish this Isle of Britain. Each century that passed, they lived longer, were better fed, better housed, used better weapons, killed off more wild beasts. They quarrelled, of course, and even killed each other; family often fought with family, tribe with tribe, for they were always breaking the Tenth Commandment. But such quarrels were not perpetual; tribe might often join with tribe, and so begin to form one nation or people. How they were governed, what their laws and customs were, what their religious ideas were, we can only guess. Perhaps the eldest man of the tribe was a sort of king and declared what were the "customs" which the tribe must keep; said "this would make the gods angry" and that would not; settled the disputes about a sheep or piece of corn-land; led the tribe to fight in battle. Perhaps this king pretended to be descended from the gods, and his tribe got to believe it.

Their tribes.

Their kings.

Who were the gods? Sun, moon, stars, rivers, trees, lakes; the rain, the lightning, the clouds; perhaps certain animals; dead ancestors, if they had been brave men, would come to be counted gods. But all round you were

Their gods.

gods and spirits of some sort whom you must
appease by sacrifices, or by absurd customs.
"Do not cut your hair by moonlight, or the
goddess of the moon will be angry." "If
you are the king, never cut your hair at all."
"Luck" perhaps was the origin of many of
such customs; some famous man *had* once
cut his hair by moonlight, and next day he had
been struck by lightning. Then there were
priests, or "medicine-men" of some kind.
These would generally support the king; but
they would often bully him also, and try to
make him enforce absurd customs.

Their
buildings.

And so the ages rolled along, and these
"Cave men" or "Stone Age men" began to
thin the forests a little or took advantage of
the clearings caused by forest fires. They
began to come down from the hill-tops, on
which their earliest homes had been made,
into the valleys. They began to come out of
their caves, and began to build themselves
villages of little wooden huts; they began to
make regular beaten track-ways along the
slopes of the downs; they began, perhaps, to
raise huge stone temples to their heathen gods.
Was it they who built Stonehenge, whose ruins
even now strike us with wonder and terror?

Their
trade with
foreigners.

Tribe began to exchange its goods with
tribe; the flints of Sussex for the deer horns of

Devon, for deer horns make excellent pickaxes.
Foreign traders came too, to buy the skins of
the wild animals, also perhaps to buy slaves.
Our ancestors were quite willing to sell their
fellow men, captives taken in war from other
tribes. What these foreigners brought in
return is not very clear; perhaps only toys and
ornaments, such as we now sell to savages;
perhaps casks of strong drink; perhaps a few
metal tools and weapons. For in Southern
Europe men had now begun to make tools and
weapons of bronze; the day of stone axes was
nearly over. So by degrees the Stone Age men
of Britain learned that there were richer and
more civilized men than themselves living
beyond the seas, who had things which they
lacked; and, as they coveted such things, they
had to make or catch something to buy them
with. Therefore they bred more big dogs,
killed and skinned more deer, caught more
slaves. So trade began in Britain, and its
benefits came first to those dwellers of the
southern and south-eastern coasts who were
nearest to the ports of Europe.

But the foreign traders also took home with
them the report that Britain looked a fertile
country, and was quite worth conquering.
And so, perhaps about a thousand years before
Christ, a set of new tribes began to cross the

Perhaps 3,000 years ago.

Coming of the Celts.

Channel, and to land in our islands, not as
traders, but as fighters. Terrible big fellows
they were, with fair hair, and much stronger
than the Stone Age men. They were armed,
too, with this new-fangled bronze, which made
short work of our poor little bows and flint-
tipped arrows and spears. Those of us who
were not killed or made slaves at once fled to
the forests, fled ever northward or westward,
or hid in our caves again. But many of us
were made slaves, especially the women, some
of whom afterward married their conquerors.
The Celts, for that was the name of the new
people, seized all the best land, all the flocks
and herds, and all the strong places on the hill-
tops, and began to lead in Britain the life which
they had been leading for several centuries
in the country we now call France. From
these Celts the Scottish, Irish, and Welsh
people are mainly descended.

Life of the   They rode on war-ponies, and, like the
Celts.   Assyrians in the Bible, they drove war-chariots;
they knew, or were soon taught by foreign
traders, how to dig in the earth for minerals,
and they soon did a large trade in that valuable
metal, tin, which is found in Cornwall, They
were in every way more civilized than the Stone
Age men; their gods were fiercer and stronger;
their priests, called Druids, more powerful;

their tribes were much larger and better organized for war. Their methods of hunting and fishing, of agriculture, of sheep and cow breeding, were much better; their trade with their brothers in France was far greater. Before they, in their turn, were conquered, they had found out the use of iron for tools and weapons; flint had gone down before bronze; so now bronze, which is a soft metal and takes time to make, rapidly went down before the cheap and hard gray iron. He who has the best tools will win in the fight with Nature; he who has the best weapons will beat his fellow men in battle.

Meanwhile, far away in the East, great empires had been growing up and decaying for six or seven thousand years. Each contributed something to civilization, Egypt, Assyria, Babylon, Persia, Greece; each in turn made a bid for conquering and civilizing the "known world." But the world that they knew stretched little beyond the warm and tideless Mediterranean Sea. After all these arose the mighty empire of Rome, the heiress and conqueror of all these civilizations and empires. Rome brought to her task a genius for war and government which none of them had known. The Roman armies had passed in conquest into Spain, into France, and from

Growth of empires in distant lands

Rome.

Caesar's invasion of Britain, 55, 54 B.C.

France they passed to Britain. The greatest of Roman soldiers, Caius Julius Caesar, who was conquering the Celts in France, landed somewhere in Kent, about fifty years before Christ's birth. He found it a tough job to struggle up to the Thames, which he crossed a little above London; tough almost as much because of the forests as because of the valiant Britons, although in the open field these were no match for the disciplined Roman regiments called "legions." It is this Caesar who wrote the first account of our island and our people which has come down to us. He was very much astonished at the tide which he found in the Channel; and his book leaves us with the impression that the spirit of the dear motherland had breathed valour and cunning in defence into the whole British people.

Second Roman Invasion A.D. 43.

For ninety years after his raid no Roman armies came to the island. But Roman traders came and Romanized Celts from France, who laughed at the "savage" ways of the British Celts. Men began to talk, in the wooden or wattle huts of British Kings (hitherto believed by the Britons to be the most magnificent buildings imaginable), of the name and fame of the great empire, of streets paved with marble, and of houses roofed with gilded bronze; of the invincible Roman legions clad

THE LANDING OF THE ROMANS

in steel and moving like steel machines; of
the great paved roads driven like arrows over
hill and dale, through the length and breadth
of Western Europe, of the temples and baths,
of the luxurious waterways of the South.
Rome attracted and terrified many peoples,
even before she conquered them. The Roman
Emperor seemed to men who had never seen
him to be a very god upon earth.

But the Roman conquest began in earnest
in the year 43, and within half a century was
fairly complete. At first it was cruel; Roman
soldiers were quite pitiless; for those who
resisted they had only the sword or slavery.
The north and west of Britain resisted long and
hard and often. Once under the great Queen
Boadicea, whose statue now stands on West-
minister Bridge in London, the Britons cut to
pieces a whole Roman legion. Then came
cruel vengeance and reconquest; but, after
reconquest, came such peace and good government as Britain had never seen before. The
Romans introduced into all their provinces a
system of law so fair and so strong that almost
all the best laws of modern Europe have been
founded on it. Everywhere the weak were
protected against the strong; castles were
built on the coast, with powerful garrisons in
them; fleets patrolled the Channel and the

The
Roman
Conquest.

The Peace
that Rome
gave.

North Sea. Great roads crossed the island
from east to west and from north to south.
Great cities, full of all the luxuries of the South,
grew up. Temples were built to the Roman
gods; and country-houses of rich Roman gentlemen, of which you may still see the remains
here and there. These gentlemen at first
talked about exile, shivered and cursed the
"beastly British climate," heated their houses
with hot air, and longed to get home to Italy.
But many stayed; their duty or their business
obliged them to stay: and into them too the
spirit of the dear motherland entered and
became a passion. Their children, perhaps,
never saw Rome; but Rome and Britain had an
equal share of their love and devotion, and
they, perhaps, thought something like this:

THE ROMAN CENTURION SPEAKS

A Roman
soldier
who loves
Britain.

Legate, I had the news last night. My cohort's
    ordered home,
By ship to Portus Itius and thence by road to
    Rome.
I've marched the companies aboard, the arms
    are stowed below:
Now let another take my sword. Command
    me not to go!

I've served in Britain forty years, from Vectis
    to the Wall
I have none other home than this, nor any
    life at all.
Last night I did not understand, but, now the
    hour draws near
That calls me to my native land, I feel that
    land is here.

Here where men say my name was made,
    here where my work was done,
Here where my dearest dead are laid — my
    wife — my wife and son;
Here where time, custom, grief and toil, age,
    memory, service, love,
Have rooted me in British soil. Ah, how
    shall I remove?

For me this land, that sea, these airs, those
    folk and fields suffice.
What purple Southern pomp can match our
    changeful Northern skies,
Black with December snows unshed or pearled
    with August haze,
The clanging arch of steel-gray March, or June's
    long-lighted days?

You'll follow widening Rhodanus till vine and
    olive lean

Aslant before the sunny breeze that sweeps
　　　Nemausus clean
To Arelate's triple gate; but let me linger on,
Here where our stiff-necked British oaks con-
　　　front Euroclydon!

You'll take the old Aurelian Road through
　　　shore-descending pines
Where, blue as any peacock's neck, the Tyr-
　　　rhene Ocean shines.
You'll go where laurel crowns are won, but
　　　will you e'er forget
The scent of hawthorn in the sun, or bracken
　　　in the wet?

Let me work here for Britain's sake — at any
　　　task you will —
A marsh to drain, a road to make, or native
　　　troops to drill.
Some Western camp (I know the Pict) or
　　　granite Border keep,
Mid seas of heather derelict, where our old
　　　mess-mates sleep.

Legate, I come to you in tears — my cohort
　　　ordered home!
I've served in Britain forty years. What
　　　should I do in Rome?

Here is my heart, my soul, my mind — the
    only life I know—
I cannot leave it all behind.   Command me
    not to go!

And peace was imposed all over Southern
Britain; and the legions came to be stationed
only on the frontier, and hardly ever moved.
No doubt at first these legions were recruited
from all the regions over which Rome ruled,
and she ruled from Euphrates to Tyne, from
Rhine to Africa.   Soon, however, they must
have been recruited in Britain itself and from
Britons.   Celtic mothers bore British sons to
Roman fathers, and crooned Celtic songs over
the cradles of babies who would one day carry
the Roman flag.   The beautiful Latin tongue,
which the Romans had brought with them,
was enriched with many Celtic words.

Mixture of British and Roman races.

It was, however, a misfortune for Britain
that Rome never conquered the whole island.
The great warrior Agricola did, between A.D.
79 and 85, penetrate far into Scotland; but he
could leave no traces of civilization behind him,
and Ireland he never touched at all.   So
Ireland never went to school, and has been a
spoilt child ever since.   And there was always
a "Scottish frontier" to be guarded, and along
this frontier the Emperor Hadrian, early in

What Rome failed to do.

the second century, began the famous Roman Wall. His successors improved on it until it became a mighty rampart of stone, eighty miles long, from Tyne to Solway, with ditches in front and behind and a strong garrison kept in its watch-towers.

The Roman Wall.

To the north of the wall roamed, almost untouched, certainly unsubdued, the wilder Celts whom the Romans called "Picts" or painted men; the screen of the wall seemed a perfectly sufficient defence against these. But prosperity and riches are often bad for men; they lead to the neglect of defence. I fear that Roman Britain went to sleep behind her walls, recruiting fell off, the strength of the legions became largely a "paper strength."

Decay of Roman power after 300 A. D.

And not only in Britain. The greatest empire that the world has ever seen was slowly dying at the heart, dying of too much power, too much prosperity, too much luxury. What a lesson for us all to-day! There were pirates abroad, who smelt plunder afar off, land-thieves and sea-thieves. They began to break through the frontiers. One fine day the terrible news came to York, the capital of Roman Britain, that the Picts were over the wall. Where was the commander-in-chief? Oh! he was at Bath taking the waters to cure his indigestion. Where was the prefect (the highest

Invasions of the Picts.

THE BUILDING OF THE WALL

representative of the Emperor)? Oh! he lived at Lyons in Southern France; for he governed France as well as Britain. Quite possibly he was actually in rebellion against the Emperor of Rome, and was thinking of marching down to Italy to make himself Emperor! If so, he would be for withdrawing the few soldiers that were left in Britain instead of sending more to defend it. "A few barbarians more or less over the wall" mattered very little to a man who lived, by neglecting his duties, in Southern France; "they could easily be driven back next year."

But it soon came to be less easy, and the barbarians soon came to be more than a few. An officer, called the "Count of the Saxon Shore," was created to watch against the pirates. The cities of Britain, hitherto undefended by fortifications, hastily began to run up walls for themselves. One day even these walls were in vain. Rome, Britain, and civilization were equally coming to an end, and it would be long before they revived. Half a century had completed the Roman conquest of the island; two and a half centuries of happy peace had followed; in another half century it was all over. Long before the last Roman legions were withdrawn, in 407, pirates had been breaking down all the walls and defences of Britain.

Fall of Roman Britain.

The English Pirates from North Germany about A.D. 350-450.

Celtic Picts from the North, Celtic Scots from Ireland; worse than all, *down the North-east wind* came terrible "Englishmen," "Saxons," from the shores of North Germany and Denmark. Rome had forced the wolf and the eagle to content themselves with rabbits and lambs; now they were going to feast once more upon the corpses of men.

CHAPTER II

SAXON ENGLAND

The Pirates in England

When Rome was rotten-ripe to her fall,
 And the sceptre passed from her hand,
The pestilent Picts leaped over the wall
 To harry the British land.

The little dark men of the mountain and waste,
 So quick to laughter and tears,
They came panting with hate and haste
 For the loot of five hundred years.

They killed the trader, they sacked the shops,
 They ruined temple and town —
They swept like wolves through the standing
  crops
 Crying that Rome was down.

They wiped out all that they could find
 Of beauty and strength and worth,
But they could not wipe out the Viking's Wind,
 That brings the ships from the North.

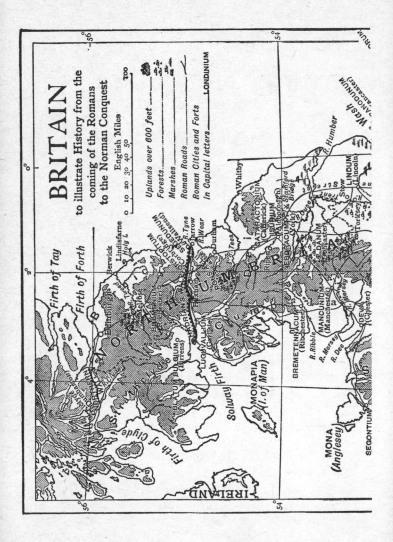

BRITAIN

to illustrate History from the
coming of the Romans
to the Norman Conquest

English Miles

0 10 20 30 40 50   100

Uplands over 600 feet ⎯⎯⎯⎯
Forests ⎯⎯⎯⎯⎯⎯⎯⎯
Marshes ⎯⎯⎯⎯⎯⎯⎯
Roman Roads ⎯⎯⎯⎯⎯⎯
Roman Cities and Forts ⎯⎯
In Capital letters ⎯ LONDINIUM

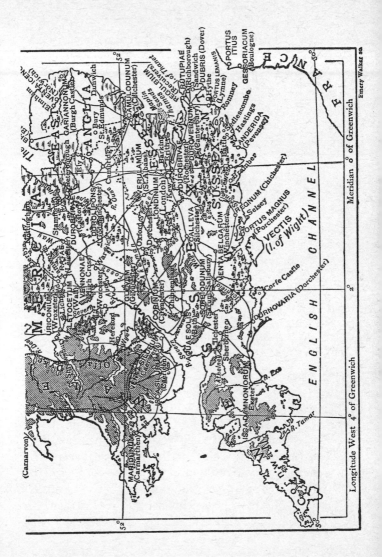

Emery Walker sc.

They could not wipe out the North-east gales,
　Nor what those gales set free —
The pirate ships with their close-reefed sails,
　Leaping from sea to sea.

They had forgotten the shield-hung hull
　Seen nearer and more plain,
Dipping into the troughs like a gull,
　And gull-like rising again —

The painted eyes that glare and frown,
　In the high snake-headed stem,
Searching the beach while her sail comes down,
　They had forgotten them!

There was no Count of the Saxon Shore
　To meet her hand to hand,
As she took the beach with a surge and a roar,
　And the pirates rushed inland.

The
British
Chris-
tians.
EARLY in the fourth century the Roman
Empire had become Christian. And among
the benefits Rome had brought to Britain was
the preaching of the Gospel. We know very
little about the old British Church, except the
names of several martyrs who died for the
faith before the conversion of the Empire.
One of these was the soldier, St. Alban, to
whom the greatest abbey in England was

afterward dedicated. It is probable, however, that, as in other parts of the Roman Empire, Britain was divided in bishoprics, churches were built, and heathen temples pulled down.

Our English and Saxon friends, when they first landed in Kent and Eastern Britain, were violent — you might almost say conscientious — heathens. They feared and hated Christianity and all other traces of Roman civilization; and they rooted out everything Roman that they could lay hands on. Other provinces of the Empire, Italy, France and Spain, were also being overrun by barbarians, but none of these was as remorseless and destructive as the Saxons. Therefore in Italy, France, and Spain the "re-making" of nations on the ruins of Rome began fairly soon, but not in Britain. The Saxons made a clean sweep of the eastern half of the island, from the Forth to the Channel and westward to the Severn. An old British chronicle gives us a hint of the awful thoroughness with which they worked. "Some therefore of the miserable remnant (of Britons) being taken in the mountains were murdered in great numbers, others constrained by famine came and yielded themselves to be slaves forever to their foes, running the risk of being instantly slain, which truly was the greatest favour that could be offered

The
Heathen
Saxons
and
English.

them: some others passed beyond the seas with loud lamentations."

The Saxon Conquest A.D. 400-600.

The Saxons brought their wives and children with them, though it is difficult to believe that they were so stupid as to kill *all* the Britons instead of enslaving them and marrying their wives. Yet, if they had not done this, surely there would have been some traces left of Latin or Celtic speech, law, and religion. But there were none. When, in the eighth and ninth centuries, we begin to see a little into the darkness, we find that England has become a purely English country, with a purely English and rather absurd system of law, and a purely English language; while, as for religion, the people have to be converted all over again by a special mission from the Pope at Rome.

Ruin of civilization.

Probably the British made a very desperate defence, and were only slowly beaten westward into Wales, Lancashire, Devon, and Cornwall. Something like two centuries passed before the English were thorough masters of the eastern half of the island. And all that while Roman temples, churches, roads, and cities were crumbling away and grass was growing over their ruins. Studying the history of those days is like looking at a battlefield in a fog. As the fog clears we get some notion of our dear barbarian forefathers.

The Saxon Englishman was a savage, with the vices and cruelties of an overgrown boy; a drunkard and a gambler, and very stupid. But he was a truth-teller, a brave, patient, and cool-headed fellow. A Roman historian describes him as "a free-necked man married to a white-armed woman who can hit as hard as horses kick." He honoured his women and he loved his home; and the spirit of the land entered into him, even more than into any of those who lived before or came after him. He never knew when he was beaten, and so he took a lot of beating. He was not quarrelsome by nature, and, indeed, when he had once settled down in Britain, he was much too apt, as his descendants are to-day, to neglect soldiering altogether. He forgot his noble trade of sailor, which had brought him to Britain, so completely that within two centuries his coasts were at the mercy of every sea-thief in Europe; and down the north-east wind the sea-thieves were always coming. England should always beware of the north-east wind. It blows her no good.

Tilling the fields was the Saxon's real job; he was a plough-boy and a cow-boy by nature, and like a true plough- and cow-boy he was always grumbling. He hated being governed; he always stood up for his "rights," and often

Life of the Saxons.

The Saxon plough-boy.

talked a lot of nonsense about them. He obeyed his kings when he pleased, which was not often, and these kings had very little power over him. But he loved his land, and he grubbed deep into it with his clumsy plough. In the sweat of his brow he ate the bread and pork and drank the beer (too much of the beer) which he raised on it.

A Saxon village. Every English village could keep itself to itself, since it produced nearly everything its people wanted, except salt, iron, and millstones, which could only be found in certain favoured places. In most villages there was a sort of squire called a "thegn," who paid something, either a rent or a service of some kind, to a king or to a bigger thegn, and owned much more land than the ordinary freemen. Probably also he owned a few slaves, whether of English or British birth. There was also a smith and a miller, a swineherd to take the village pigs into the forest to feed, a shepherd and a cowherd, and a doctor who would be more or less of a wizard. After the conversion to Christianity in the seventh century there was also in most villages a priest. Of the freemen, every head of a family owned certain strips of land on which he grew corn, and each helped his neighbour to plough the land with teams of oxen. There was also a great common on which all freemen could pasture their cattle, and a wood wherein the pigs fed. There were few horses, there was no hay to feed them on, cows were only killed for food when they were too old to draw the plough, sheep were chiefly kept for wool, and so the pig was the real friend of hungry men.

There was in each district some sort of rude government by some sort of rude king, whose ancestor may have been a leading pirate of the first ship-load of Saxons who landed near that place. No doubt many tiny "kingdoms" sprang up, as ship-load after ship-load of pirates explored and settled inland. Probably the first "kingdoms" extended as far as an armed man could walk before a day's honest fighting, but these would naturally melt into or be conquered into larger territories. In the seventh century there were at least seven little kingdoms, but, by the eighth, only three of any importance remained: *The small Saxon kingdoms.*

1. Northumbria, stretching from the Forth to the Humber, and westward to the hills that part Cumberland and Lancashire from Yorkshire and Northumberland. *The three large Saxon kingdoms.*

2. Mercia, or Middle England, reaching from the Humber to the Thames and westward to the Severn.

3. Wessex, comprising all south of the Thames and as far west as Devon.

When they were tired of fighting the Britons, the kings of these small kingdoms constantly fought each other.

Their government; their gods.

There were laws, or, rather, deeply rooted "customs," mostly connected with fighting, or cows or ploughing. There were rude courts of justice, which would fine a man so many sheep or so many silver pennies for murder or wounding or cow-stealing. The king had a council of "wise men," who met in his wooden house to advise him, and to drink with him afterward at his rude feasts. There were gods, called Tiu and Woden and Thor and Freya, from whom our Tuesday, Wednesday, Thursday and Friday are derived. They lived in a heaven called Valhalla, where, our ancestors thought, there was an endless feast of pork and strong ale, with no headaches to follow.

A barbarous freedom.

All this, as you see, was a barbarous business, after the well-organized, civilized Roman life; but at least it was a life with a good deal of freedom in it. Rome had stifled freedom too much; the Saxons went to the other extreme. It is quite possible to have too much freedom, and you will see what a price these Saxons, before the end of their six hundred years of freedom, had to pay for theirs.

After the sack of the City when Rome was
    sunk to a name,
In the years when the lights were darkened,
    or ever St. Wilfred came,
Low on the borders of Britain (the ancient
    poets sing)
Between the cliff and the forest there ruled a
    Saxon King.

Stubborn were all his people from cotter
    to overlord,
Not to be cowed by the cudgel, scarce to be
    schooled by the sword,
Quick to turn at their pleasure, cruel to cross
    in their mood,
And set on paths of their choosing as the hogs
    of Andred's Wood.

Laws they made in the Witan, the laws of
    flaying and fine —
Common, loppage and pannage, the theft
    and the track of kine,
Statues of tun and of market for the fish and
    the malt and the meal,
The tax on the Bramber packhorse, and the
    tax on the Hastings keel.
Over the graves of the Druids and under the
    wreck of Rome,
Rudely but surely they bedded, the plinth
    of the days to come.

The Saxon foundations of England.

Behind the feet of the Legions and before
  the Normans' ire,
Rudely but greatly begat they the bones of
  state and of shire;
Rudely but deeply they laboured, and their
  labour stands till now,
If we trace on our ancient headlands, the
  twist of their eight-ox plough.

Growth of
great land-
owners.

There was no king really powerful enough
to rule the whole island. In a land of forest
and swamp, where roads hardly exist for eight
months of the year, it must always be difficult
for armed men, judges or traders to pass from
place to place, except on horseback; and the
Saxons were no great horse-soldiers. I think
we shall see that it was the knight and his horse,
who, from the eleventh century onward, first
made the rule of one king possible over the
whole island. Meanwhile, the "great men"
of the Saxons, "thegns," "aldermen," "earls,"
or whatever they were called, took most of
the power, and naturally began to oppress
their poorer neighbours. They got the courts
of justice into their own hands; they grabbed
the land, they exacted rents and services from
the poorer landowners; they made what is
called a "feudal" state of society. In the
year 600 a free Kentish farmer might own 120

acres of land; in the year 1000 he seldom owned more than 30, and for this he probably had to pay a heavy rent and to labour on some great man's land.

The first rudiments of civilization were brought back to this barbarous England by the Christian missionaries whom Pope Gregory sent thither in the year 597. St. Augustine came and preached in Kent and became the first Archbishop of Canterbury. From Canterbury missionaries spread all over the island, and, in a century, the heathenism that had rooted out Christianity two hundred years before was quite gone. It seems that the fierce Saxon gods made a very poor fight of it. The old Roman capital of York recovered its importance and became an archbishopric. Some seventeen other bishoprics arose all over the country, and, even more important than the bishoprics, great abbeys and monasteries full of monks and nuns. A monk is a person who retires from the world in order to devote himself to prayer with a view to saving his own soul.

Besides preaching the true Gospel of our Lord, these missionaries preached the worship of saints, and every church was dedicated to some particular saint, who was believed to watch over its congregation. A gift of land

The Saxons become Christian after A.D. 597.

Bishops and monks.

Gifts of land to the monks.

to a monastery was called "a gift to God and
His saints." If you were not holy enough to
go into the monastery, the next best thing you
could do, said the monks, was to give your
land to the saints. But this meant that you
neglected your worldly duties, such as defending your country, tilling your fields, providing
for your wife and children. The world, in
fact, was painted to our Saxon ancestors by
the monks as such a terribly wicked place
that the best thing they could do was to get
Power of out of it as quickly as possible. The Popes
the Pope. of Rome, who had about this time made themselves supreme heads of all Western Christendom, encouraged this view; and the monks
were always devoted servants of the Popes.
But there were other priests who were not
monks, and these usually served the parish
churches, which gradually but slowly grew up
in England; they were always rather jealous
of the monks.

Life of the   Human love and common sense were too
monks. strong to be taken in altogether by this new
unworldly spirit. Even the monks themselves
soon became very human, and, as they had to
eat and drink, they had to cultivate their
fields to raise food. Indeed, they soon began
to do this more intelligently than most people;
and so the monasteries became very rich.

ST. AUGUSTINE PREACHING TO ETHELBERT

I think it is to the monks that we English owe our strong love of gardening and flowers; and also our love of fishing. The Church said you were to eat only fish and eggs in the season of Lent and on other "fast-days," and so every monastery, however far from a river, had to have a fish-pond well stocked with fish, or else live upon salt herrings, which were difficult to get far inland. I always like to think of the dear old monks, in their thick, black woollen frocks, with their sleeves tucked up, watching their floats in the pond. I hope they were always strictly truthful as to the size of the fish which they hooked but did not land. The monks also kept alive what remains of learning there were: they brought books from beyond the seas; they taught schools; made musical instruments, were builders, painters, and craftsmen of all kinds; and produced famous men of learning like Bede and Wilfred. English missionaries went from English abbeys to preach the Gospel to heathen Germans. So rich and powerful did the Church become that in the councils of our tenth-century kings the bishops and abbots were even more important than the thegns and earls.

The Church then taught men much and tamed them a little. It certainly helped toward uniting the jarring kingdoms; for

Power of the Kings of Northumbria, 630-750.

Christian Northumbria, in the seventh century, was the first to exercise a real sort of leadership over the other kingdoms; it was a Northumbrian king, Edwin, who built and gave his name to Edinburgh; it was in the Northumbrian monastery of Jarrow that the good monk Bede wrote the first history of England. You may still see Bede's tomb in Durham Cathedral, with the Latin rhyme on the great stone lid. The last important Northumbrian king fell fighting against the Picts beyond the Forth.

Kings of Mercia, 750-800. Mercia had her turn of supremacy in the eighth century, under King Offa, who drove back the Welsh and took in a lot of their land beyond the Severn. Perhaps it was he who built a great rampart there called Offa's Dyke; beyond it, even to this day, all is "Wales."

Egbert, King of Wessex, 802. Then his family in turn was beaten by Egbert, King of Wessex (802-39). Thenceforth, Wessex was, in name at least, supreme over all England. If ever there was a capital city of England before Norman times it was Winchester, the chief town of Wessex; though London, one of the few Roman cities that have never been destroyed or left desolate, must always have been a more important place of trade. *From Egbert King George V is directly descended!*

New Pirates from Denmark and Norway, 800-1100. Egbert and his son and grandsons had to meet a new and terrible foe. Down to the

north-east wind, from Denmark, Norway, and
the Baltic, all through the ninth, tenth, and
eleventh centuries, a continual stream of fierce
and cunning pirates began to pour upon
Western Europe. We call them "the Danes,"
or North-men. The British Isles lay right
in their path, and at one time or another they
harried them from end to end. The churches,
in which the principal wealth of the country
was stored, were sacked; the monks were killed,
and then the pirates went back to their ships.
From Britain they went on to France and even
into the Mediterranean: some of them, indeed,
crossed the Northern Ocean to Iceland, to
Greenland, to North America. Their ships,
some 80 feet long, and 16 feet broad, with a
draught of 4 feet, might carry crews of fifty men
apiece, armed to the teeth in shirts of mail,
and bearing heavy axes with shafts as long as
a man. Often they came under pretence of
trading in slaves, and would trade honestly
enough if they thought the country too strong
to be attacked. About the middle of the
ninth century they began to settle and make
homes in the very lands they had been plundering. Lincolnshire, Nottinghamshire, the East
Riding of Yorkshire were regularly colonized
by them. So were the Orkney and Shetland
Isles, the Hebrides, Caithness, and Sutherland,

These
Pirates
begin to
settle in
England
about 860.

as well as the Isle of Man and the eastern coast of Ireland.

Their numbers were, however, small, and if Saxon England under weak kings had not enjoyed too much "freedom," they might have been beaten off; but it seemed impossible for the Saxons to collect an army in less than a month, or to keep it in the field when collected. Long before the English "host" was ready to fight, the pirates had harried the land and disappeared. At last Alfred the Great (871–901), grandson of Egbert, began to turn the tide against the invaders. He defended Wessex all along the line of the Upper Thames, in battle after desperate battle, and at last beat a big Danish army somewhere in Wiltshire. The pirate king Guthrum agreed to become a Christian, and was allowed to settle with his men in North-eastern England. Soon after that we find English and "settled" Danes fighting valiantly for their country against fresh bands of Danish pirates. We may call Alfred the first real "King of England"; he picked up the threads of the national life which the Danes had cut to pieces. He translated good books into the Saxon tongue; he started the great history of England, called the "Chronicle," which was kept year by year, in more than one monastery, down to 1154. He and his son

Alfred the Great saves Southern England, 871-901.

The great Kings of Wessex of the tenth century.

Edward, and his grandsons Athelstan and Edmund, built fleets and fortresses, armed their people afresh and compelled them to fight in their own defence. For some years every fresh band of pirates met a warm reception and every rising of the Danes within the country was beaten down. King Edgar, 959–75, was called "The Peaceful," and boasted that he had been rowed about on the river Dee by six lesser kings.

It was a brief respite,

> For all about the shadowy kings,
> Denmark's grim ravens cowered their
>   wings;

and in the reign of Edgar's foolish son, Ethelred the Unready, the pirates came back more determined than before. Sweyn, king of Denmark, came in person, and his son Canute; and this time the Danes intended a thorough and wholesale conquest. This time Wessex fell also; even Canterbury was sacked, and its archbishop pelted to death with beef-bones after dinner. The "wise men" of unwise Ethelred were as useless as the House of Commons would be to-day if there were a big invasion. They talked, but did nothing. A country in such a plight wants a *man* to lead it to war; not thirty "wise men" or six hundred mem-

King Ethelred the Unready, 979–1016; fresh Danish raids.

bers of Parliament, with a sprinkling of traitors among them, to discuss how to make peace. Ethelred's "wise men" could only recommend him to buy off the Danes with hard cash called "Danegold" or "Dane-geld." The Danes pocketed the silver pennies, laughed, and came back for more. When for a moment there arose a hero, Ethelred's son, Edmund Ironside, he fought in one year, as Alfred had fought, six pitched battles and almost beat Canute. Then he agreed to divide the island with Canute, and was murdered in the next year (1017). Canute ruled England until his death in 1053. He ruled Denmark and Norway also, and was in fact a sort of Northern Emperor.

The "Dane-geld."

King Canute, 1016-1035.

What "Dane-geld" means.

It is always a temptation to an armed and agile nation
    To call upon a neighbour and to say:
"We invaded you last night — we are quite prepared to fight,
    Unless you pay us cash to go away."

    And that is called asking for Dane-geld,
        And the people who ask it explain
    That you've only to pay 'em the Dane-geld
        And then you'll get rid of the Dane!

It is always a temptation to a rich and lazy
  nation
To puff and look important and to say:
"Though we know we should defeat you, we
  have not the time to meet you,
We will therefore pay you cash to go away."

And that is called paying the Dane-geld;
  But we've proved it again and again,
That if once you have paid him the
  Dane-geld
You never get rid of the Dane!

It is wrong to put temptation in the path of
  any nation,
For fear they should succumb and go astray,
So when you are requested to pay up or be
  molested,
You will find it better policy to say:

"We never pay any one Dane-geld,
  No matter how trifling the cost,
For the end of that game is oppression
  and shame,
And the nation that plays it is lost!"

And Canute ruled England righteously. He
turned Christian, he rebuilt the abbeys and
churches which his ancestors had burned, he

kept a strong little army of English or Danish soldiers about his person, and he kept order and peace. His sons, however, were good for

King Edward the Confessor, 1042-1066. nothing; and in 1042 Edward, the younger son of Ethelred, was recalled from "Normandy," whither he had been sent to be out of Canute's way, and ruled England as king till 1066.

Dangers from abroad. Now, as we approach the end of the Saxon period of our history let us take a look at our foreign neighbours. Those who will be important to us are four in number.

1. Denmark and Norway; except in the reign of Canute, these were always hostile.

Scotland. 2. Scotland, once Pict-land, the district north of the Forth and Clyde. Celtic "Scots" from Ireland had conquered Celtic Picts from the sixth to the ninth century. They had brought with them the Christian faith, which had been preached in Ireland by St. Patrick in the fifth century. These Scots and Picts continually raided Northumbria, just as the Picts had raided Roman Britain; and Canute had bought off their raids by giving to them all the land as far south as the Tweed, which thus became the "border," as we have it to-day, between England and Scotland. Cumberland and Lancashire seem to have remained an independent Celtic country till the end of the eleventh century, just as Wales did till the thirteenth.

3. Flanders, that is, roughly speaking, the Flanders.
modern Holland and Belgium; a land already
famous both for pirates and traders; it lies
right opposite the mouth of the Thames, and
was just the place where the pirates could sell
the gold candlesticks which they stole out
of English churches.

4. Normandy, the great province on the Normandy and the Normans.
north coast of France, of which the river Seine
is the centre. This land the great Danish
pirate, Rollo, had harried early in the tenth
century, until the wearied King of France gave
it him to keep, on condition that he would
become a Christian. The "Normans," that
is North-men, married French wives, and
became the cleverest, the fiercest, and, according to the ideas of the day, the most pious
of Frenchmen. They did not cease to be
adventurers, and we find their young men
seeking their fortunes all over Europe. They
thought their Saxon neighbours very slow and
stupid fellows, who were somehow in possession
of a very desirable island which they managed
very badly, and which it was the Norman's
duty to take if possible.

Now King Edward was at heart more a Duke William.
Norman than an Englishman, so pious that he
was called "the Confessor," always confessing
sins that he had not committed, and for-

getting his real sin, which was the neglect of the defence of his island. Like the Normans, he despised his own people. He gave himself away to his young cousin, Duke William of Normandy, and would have liked to give the crown and land of England as well — in fact, he made some sort of promise to do so — and he filled his court with Norman favourites and bishops. England had never yet been a united country. Ethelred, and Canute after him, had allowed great "aldermen" or earls to govern it, one for Northumbria, one for Mercia, one for Wessex; Edward continued the same plan, and so these great earls were more powerful than the King himself. Northumbria and Mercia were largely Danish at heart and looked more to Denmark than to Wessex for a king. It was on Wessex, then, that the main resistance to Normandy would fall if the Normans attacked England.

Earl Harold of Wessex.

Becomes King, 1066.

Invasions prepared from Norway and Normandy.

Edward had no children, and as he drew toward his death, the great Earl Harold of Wessex had to make up his mind whether he would submit to Duke William of Normandy, or call in Danish help, or seize the crown of England for himself. Ambition and patriotism both said "Seize it"; and on Edward's death, in January 1066, Harold did so.

Danes and Norwegians were on the alert

too; and it looked as if England might be crushed between two sets of enemies. For William had long been preparing for a spring at it: he had won the friendship of Flanders; and he had the Pope on his side, for the English Church was by no means too obedient to the Pope at this time. William now set about collecting a great army of the best fighting men that France, Brittany, and Flanders could produce. Our brave Harold, on his side, got the Wessex men under arms, and kept them watching all the summer. Northern England could not help him, for, a month before William landed from France, a mighty Norwegian host appeared in the Humber.

Harold, then, had to prepare to meet two invasions; and most gallantly he met them. He flew to York, smashed the Norwegians to pieces at Stamford Bridge, and flew south again: but before he reached London William had landed in Sussex. There, upon October 14th, on or near the spot where Battle Abbey now stands, was fought the Battle of Hastings, one of the most decisive battles in history. It was the fight of French cavalry and archers against the English and Danish foot-soldiers and axe-men, a fight of valour and cunning against valour without cunning. All day they fought, till, in the autumn darkness, the last

Battle of Stamford Bridge, 1066, September.

Battle of Hastings, 1066, October.

of Harold's axe-men had fallen beside their dying King, and the few English survivors had fled toward London. One of them left a bag of coins in a ditch at Sedlescombe, which was dug out a few years ago; the poor little silver pieces are a token of the many foreign countries with which Old England had dealings.

Results of the Norman Conquest.

The Battle of Hastings decided, though not even William knew it, that the great, slow, dogged English race was to be governed and disciplined (and at first severely bullied in the process) by a small number of the cleverest, strongest, most adventurous race then alive. Nothing more was wanted to make our island the greatest country in the world. The Saxons had been sinking down into a sleepy, fat, drunken, unenterprising folk. The Normans were temperate in food and drink, highly educated, as education went in those days, restless, and fiery. They brought England back by the scruff of the neck into the family of European nations, back into close touch with the Roman Church, to which a series of vigorous and clever Popes was then giving a new life. Such remains of Roman ideas of government and order as were left in Europe were saved for us by the Normans. The great Roman empire was like a ship that had been wrecked on a beach; its cargo was plundered by nation after nation. But if any nation had got the lion's share of its leavings it was the Frenchmen, and through the Frenchmen the Normans, and through the Normans the English.

It cost William about six years of utterly ruthless warfare to become master of all England. England resisted him bit by bit; its leaders had a dozen different plans; he had but one plan, and he drove it through. He was going to make an England that would resist the next invader as *one people*. He had to do terrible things: he had to harry all Yorkshire into a desert; he had to drive all the bravest English leaders into forest and fen, or over the Scottish border, and to kill them when he caught them. He spared no man who stood in his way, but he spared all who asked his mercy. He could not subdue Scotland; but once he marched to the Tay and brought the Scottish king Malcolm to his knees for the time.

The Conquest completed, 1066-1072.

William could not quite give up the plan of governing England by great earls; he was obliged to reward the most powerful of his French followers with huge grants of English land; and these followers, who had been quite accustomed to rebel against him in Normandy, often rebelled against him and his descendants in England. But his gifts of land were nearly always scattered in such a way that one great

The great Norman landowners.

man might have land perhaps in ten different counties, but not too much in any one place. Besides, every landowner, big or little, had to swear a strong oath to be faithful to the King. All gifts of land were to come only from the King, all courts of justice should depend upon the King alone. It remained for William's great-grandson Henry II to put all this down in black and white, in ink, on parchment. Henry knew, what even William had not learned, that the pen is a much more terrible and lasting recorder than the sword.

King William I. 1066-1087.

In a word, William would be King not only of Wessex but of every rood of English land and of all men dwelling thereon. And so the country began once more to enjoy a peace it had never known since the Roman legions left. The sons of the very men who had fought William at Hastings flew to fight for William against some rebel Norman earl, and earls and other men found that if they wanted to play the game of rebellion they had better go back to France. And the actual number of Normans who remained in England and took root was really very small, though among them we should find nearly all the nobles, bishops, great abbots, and other leaders of the people. Very few Norman women came, so these men married English wives, and, within

150 years, all difference between Normans and Englishmen had vanished. The Norman Conquest of 1066 was the beginning of the history of the English race as one people and of England as a great power in Europe. You might say, indeed:

England's on the anvil — hear the hammers ring —
    Clanging from the Severn to the Tyne!
Never was a blacksmith like our Norman King —
    England's being hammered, hammered, hammered into line!

England's on the anvil! Heavy are the blows!
    (But the work will be a marvel when it's done)
Little bits of kingdoms cannot stand against their foes.
    England's being hammered, hammered, hammered into one!

There shall be one people — it shall serve one Lord —
    (Neither Priest nor Baron shall escape!)
It shall have one speech and law, soul and strength and sword.
    England's being hammered, hammered, hammered into shape!

William's work.

CHAPTER III

THE NORMAN KINGS 1066-1154

The power of the kings in Norman England.

So AT last there was going to be a real government in this country, and it was going to do its duty. Few kings in the Middle Ages had any high idea of their "duty toward their people" such as a great Roman emperor had, or such as King George V has. They chiefly thought of their country as a property, or "estate," which they were going to cultivate mainly for their own benefit. *But* the better a king's "estate" was cultivated, the better off were the people on it; and, when I say the "people," I mean every one except a few, perhaps a couple of hundred of the "barons" or greatest landowners. A king could only grow very rich and powerful when his country was at peace at home and well armed against foreign foes; his people could only grow rich under the same conditions.

Their struggles with the barons, 1066-1175.

Not so the great barons. Each of them could most easily increase his riches at the expense of some other great baron or of the king; and the people who lived near him would be the first to suffer if he were allowed to do so. William had been obliged to allow his barons and earls to judge and govern their tenants in accordance with those "feudal" customs which had come to be universal in Western Europe since Roman law had been lost and strong government with it. The great kings who succeeded him slowly, painfully, out of scanty material, had to recreate a strong government, and, so, to give peace and order.

Now of the first four, whom alone we call "Norman" kings, three were wise and strong — William I, William II, and Henry I — and the fourth, Stephen, was foolish and weak. So, while the first sixty-nine years after the conquest were a time of increasing peace and prosperity, the next nineteen were the most dreadful period in our history.

Remember that the Norman barons were only five or six generations removed from the fierce Danish pirates who followed Rollo to France. There, as there were no strong kings to restrain them, they had been accustomed to build castles and to make their tenants fight for them in their private quarrels. When they got to England, and grew richer in lands and tenants than they had been in Normandy, they expected to play their familiar game with even greater success. Their kings, however, from the first, determined they should not do so.

The people will help the King against the barons.

William found, in the slow, undisciplined old Saxon life, several things which served him to keep his barons in order. For instance, there was an officer in every county called a *sheriff*; he collected the King's rents and taxes; he presided over the rude court of justice which

The Sheriffs

was held in every county; he was supposed to lead to battle the free landowners of that county. William made his sheriffs much more powerful, and made them responsible for the peace of their counties. In England, too, there had

Castles.

been few castles, and these only stockades of wood on the top of earthen mounds; whereas in France every baron had a castle. On the Welsh and Scottish borders William was obliged to allow, and even to encourage, his followers to build castles, but elsewhere he forbade it. But he built a great many *royal* castles and filled them with faithful paid soldiers. Again, in Normandy there had been barons as rich in lands and money as the Duke himself; but William kept enormous tracts of English land in his own hands, and so made the Crown ten times richer than any baron. In Normandy

Taxes.

the Duke had no real system of taxes; in England the King could and did levy a regular tax of so many shillings on each estate. Ethelred had begun this in order to get money to bribe the Danes; the later kings had continued it.

Many estates were, however, free from this Domes-
tax, and no doubt it was always difficult to day Book, 1085.
collect. So, in 1085, William sent officers to
every village and county in England to find out
who must pay the tax and how much each must
pay. These officers called together a sort of
"jury" of the villagers, who declared the value of
the estate. The results were collected and
written down in "Domesday Book," which you
may see in the British Museum. An extract
from it will run somewhat like this: "County
of Cambridge: In Blackacre are ten hides
(the hide is an old measure of land, say 120
acres). Thurstan holds it. In King Edward's
time Wulfstan held it. It was worth £2 6s. 8d.
Now it is worth £4 13s. 4d. It never paid tax.
There is land for eight ploughs. There are two
freeholders and ten serfs. The priest holds
half a hide. There is a mill, value 10s. There
is wood for 100 pigs, and pasture for 20
cows."

Are you astonished at the small value of Old
land? You must remember that you could English Money.
then buy with £1 what might now cost you
£40. For there was little silver and less gold
in Europe before the discovery of America.
Few gold coins were made in England before
the reign of Edward III.

From "Domesday Book" we can make a rough

The population of England in 1085.

guess at the population of England in the eleventh century, say about 2,000,000, whereas now it is over 40,000,000. The book does not mention the number of people in the towns, but in many towns it does mention the number of houses. Probably no town, except London, had then as many as ten thousand people. Of many places the book says that they were "waste," that is, had been burned, either by accidental fires (which must constantly have been occurring when all buildings were of wood) or by Danes or Normans in the process of conquest. It also tells something of the "customs" which prevailed in different counties and towns. We are getting near an age when we shall be able to call such customs "Laws." The Norman kings tried to use old English customs and to improve them. But theft and murder were still reckoned more as offences against the family of the person wronged than as crimes against the state. You could still atone for such offences by a fine. It was not till late in the twelfth century that you would infallibly be hanged if you were caught; and the certainty of punishment is what really prevents crime.

Customs and laws.

Free landowners and unfree tenants.

Now, you can see that the result of an inquiry like Domesday was that the kings knew a great deal about their country and about their people. They would know, for instance, what great baron or earl was really dangerous; on what part of England what taxes could be levied, and so on. No doubt the new Norman land-owners were often hard to their Saxon tenants. But it would not pay them to be too hard. They wanted rents and labour, and a starving man cannot pay rent or work in the fields. The land was the only source of riches, and therefore every gentleman had to be first and foremost a farmer, and his tenants under him had to be farmers or farm labourers too. Domesday mentions, under strange names, a great number of different classes of farming tenants; but, within the next century, we find that all these are melted away into two, the free and the unfree, the freeholders and the "villeins" or "serfs." The former are men whose land averages perhaps forty acres. They pay some small rent in money or in produce to the squire or "lord of the manor," they follow the sheriff to battle when he bids them. The villein perhaps farms nearly as much land as the freeholder. But he is not *free;* he is bound to pay a rent in labour, say two or even three days a week on the squire's land, many extra days at harvest time, and perhaps to pay so many eggs, or pigs, or hens every year; nor may he sell his land or go away without his squire's leave. In fact he is very much at the mercy of the squire until the latter half of the twelfth century, when the King's Law begins to protect him against the squire, to hang him if he commits crimes, and to enroll him as a soldier. But it will not pay the squire to oppress him too much if he is to get good work out of him. These clever Normans, all but a few of the greatest barons, soon made common cause with their tenants, soon became English at heart. Over them, too, the good land threw its dear familiar spell, and made them love it beyond all things.

NORMAN AND SAXON

Views of a Norman baron about his property. in 1100.

"My son," said the Norman Baron, "I am dying, and you will be heir
To all the broad acres in England that William gave me for my share
When we conquered the Saxon at Hastings, and a nice little handful it is.
But before you go over to rule it I want you to understand this:

"The Saxon is not like us Normans; his manners are not so polite;
But he never means anything serious till he talks about justice and right;

When he stands like an ox in the furrow with
    his sullen set eyes on your own,
And grumbles, 'This isn't fair dealing,' my son,
    leave the Saxon alone.

"You can horsewhip your Gascony archers, or
    torture your Picardy spears,
But don't try that game on the Saxon; you'll
    have the whole brood round your ears.
From the richest old Thane in the county to the
    poorest chained serf in the fields,
They'll be at you and on you like hornets, and,
    if you are wise, you will yield!

"But first you must master their language, their
    dialect, proverbs, and songs,
Don't trust any clerk to interpret when they
    come with the tale of their wrongs.
Let them know that you know what they're
    saying; let them feel that you know what
    to say;
Yes, even when you want to go hunting, hear
    them out if it takes you all day.

"They'll drink every hour of the daylight and
    poach every hour of the dark,
It's the sport, not the rabbits, they're after
    (we've plenty of game in the park).

Don't hang them or cut off their fingers.
That's wasteful as well as unkind,
For a hard-bitten, South-country poacher makes
the best man-at-arms you can find.

"Appear with your wife and the children at
their weddings and funerals and feasts;
Be polite but not friendly to bishops; be good
to all poor parish priests;
Say "we," "us," and "ours" when you're talking, instead of "you fellows" and "I."
Don't ride over seeds; keep your temper; and
never you tell 'em a lie!"

Life in the town. The towns were no doubt horrid places. The fortification of one or more "boroughs" in each county had been begun by the son and grandsons of King Alfred in their wars against the Danes. Besides a wooden castle on a mound of earth, there would probably be some sort of wooden paling round the towns; and in the twelfth century palings would be replaced by stone walls. London, York, and Chester probably kept their old Roman walls of stone and occasionally repaired them. As for cleanliness and what we now call "sanitation," there was none. All refuse was thrown into the streets, which only rainstorms washed, and where pigs, dogs, and kites scavenged freely. Each trade or craft had its own street, and a walk down "Butcher's Row" would probably be unpleasing to modern noses. But there was strong patriotism in the towns, and great rivalry between them. A townsman from Abingdon was a suspected "foreigner" to the citizens of Oxford. In Sussex to-day the old folk in some villages speak of a hop-picker from another village as a "foreigner."

Both in town and country the food, even of the poorest, was fairly plentiful. Salt meat, mainly pork, and in Lent salt fish, was the rule, and was washed down by huge floods of strong beer. There were no workhouses and no provision for the poor except charity, but charity (called "almsgiving") was universal, and beggars swarmed everywhere. If no one else would feed them, the monks always would, and I fear they made little difference between those who were really in need and those who preferred begging to working. Washing was almost unknown. Even in the King's household, while there were hundreds of servants in the cooking departments, there were only four persons in the laundry. Horrible diseases like leprosy were common, and occasionally pestilence swept away whole villages and streets of people. *The food of the people.*

Life then was undoubtedly shorter, and its conditions harder, than to-day; but I think it *The Norman Church.*

was often merrier. Holidays were much more
frequent; for the all-powerful Church forbade
work on the very numerous saints' days. Religion influenced every act of life from the cra-
dle to the grave. All the village feasts and fairs
centred round the village church and were
blessed by some saint. The Norman bishops
at once woke up the sleepy Saxon priests and
abbots, taught them to use better music, more
splendid and more frequent services, cleaner ways
of life. Stone churches replaced the w ooden
ones, and those mighty Norman cathedrals,
so much of which remains to-day, began to grow
up. The zeal for monkery continued right into
the thirteenth century, although a pious Norman gentleman seldom went into a monastery
himself till his fighting days were over. In the
Church a career was open to the poorest village
lad who was clever and industrious; he might
rise to be abbot, bishop, councillor of kings, or
even Pope. All schools were in the hands
of churchmen, and Latin was the universal
language of the Church throughout Western
Europe.

The King's Great Council. In King William's Great Council, which
took the place of the Saxon "Wise Men," and
which became the direct father of the House
of Lords, there would sit perhaps 150 great lay
barons, nineteen bishops, and some thirty

abbots; but the churchmen would be the most
learned, the most cunning and the most regular
attendants.   Though this Great Council met
only for a few days in each year, the King would
need secretaries, and lawyers, and officials of
one kind or another to be continually about his
person; and most of these would be churchmen
whom he would reward with bishoprics and
abbeys and livings.   So far as there was what
we now call a " Ministry " or a "Privy Council,"
it consisted mainly of churchmen.

So powerful indeed was the Church that
quarrels between it and the strong kings were of
frequent occurrence during the next century
or two.   The churchmen were too apt to look
to the Pope as their real head instead of the
King. The Popes always tried to keep the
Church independent of the King.   They wanted
the clergy to pay no taxes for their lands, to
have separate courts of justice, to be governed
by other laws than those of the laymen, and yet
to be wholly defended by the kings and laymen.
Now no good king approved of these demands,
which were indeed monstrous if you consider
that the clergy owned between one quarter and
one third of the land of England, and were getting more and more, from gifts by pious laymen,
every day.   William I had to grant separate
courts of justice, and he had no actual quarrel

Quarrels
of the
King with
the
Church.

with the Pope, mainly because his archbishop, Lanfranc, was a very wise man. But William II and Henry I each had sharp quarrels with Archbishop Anselm, while as for poor Stephen, he was at the mercy of the great bishops.

Task of the Norman kings. I don't think you want to know at what date this or that baron rebelled against William or Henry, or at what date William or Henry sent an army against the King of France or the Welsh; I would rather that you would understand how these kings were pursuing, on the whole, two main tasks. First, they were trying to make England and Wales one compact kingdom, and, secondly, they were obliged, because they were Dukes of Normandy, to quarrel with the Kings of France. It was they, then, who founded our 800-year-long hostility to the gallant Frenchmen, which is now, happily, at an end.

Beginnings of the Conquest of Wales. The first of these tasks was mainly left to the great Norman barons, the Earls of Chester, Shrewsbury and Gloucester, who built castles on the Welsh border and sent continual expeditions far into Wales. William II once marched himself to the foot of Snowdon, and gave the Welsh thieves a very severe lesson against stealing English cattle and murdering English settlers. Henry I started a regular colony of Englishmen in Pembrokeshire. Welsh "princes" continued to exist till the end of the thirteenth century, but only once troubled England seriously after Henry I's time.

In the North-west, William II completely conquered Westmoreland, Lancashire, and Cumberland, made them English ground forever, and rebuilt the old Roman fortress of Carlisle. On the Scottish border William I built a great fortress at Newcastle-on-Tyne; but this did not stop King Malcolm's raids, for many Saxons, who had lost their lands in 1066, had fled to Scotland and helped in these raids. But William II and Henry I managed their Scottish neighbours so cleverly that from 1095 to 1138 there were no more Scottish raids at all. During these years of peace many Norman barons got into the south of Scotland, were welcomed and were endowed with lands by King David I.

and of Cumberland;

attitude of the Norman King to Scotland.

As regards the French business, there was very little real peace between the Duke of Normandy and the French King. And as the former was now King of England also, he generally got the best of it. Until the middle of the twelfth century the King of France was very poor and could get very few people to fight for him, whereas Henry I once shipped a lot of sturdy English soldiers across the Channel and won a great victory at Tenchebray, 1106, over Norman rebels who were being aided by the

Quarrels with the King of France, 1066-1154.

French King. As a rule, however, our kings fought their battles in France with foreign soldiers hired in Flanders. The English kings even had some sort of a fleet, for the "Cinque Ports" (Dover, Sandwich, Hythe, Romney, and Hastings) were obliged to furnish them a certain number of ships every year. The causes of these quarrels with France are not interesting to us. They were usually about some frontier castle which the French King had grabbed or wanted to grab from the Duke, or the Duke from the King. At one of these quarrels William the Conqueror met his death in 1087. A terrible king and a terrible man he had been; but he had kept peace, and the fiercest baron had trembled before him. His one pleasure was hunting, and he was so greedy of it that he began to make a series of cruel laws against poachers which later kings kept up till 1217. It was death to kill a stag in the royal forests.

His eldest son, Robert, was a weak, good-natured fellow, who had once rebelled against his father, and was the darling of the turbulent barons. So William had left Normandy to Robert and England to his second son, William, who was called "Rufus" from his red hair. Rufus was a violent ruffian, grasping and cruel, and mocked at everything holy; but he was strong and clever, too, a mighty warrior and leader of

The sons of William I.

William II, called "Rufus" 1087-1100.

men. He had at once to meet a fearful rebellion got up by Robert, but the English freeholders turned out in crowds to help him, and he smashed the rebels and battered down their castles, as he battered down everything that came in his path. Soon he managed to grab Normandy also from poor Robert, who was always deep in debt and trouble of every sort.

In 1096 Robert had gone to the East, and many of the turbulent French and Norman barons with him. They had gone in order to fulfil one of the noblest yet vainest dreams of those times, to rescue the Holy Land from the infidel Saracens or "Turks," who had recently taken Jerusalem. The Saracens bullied pilgrims who went thither to venerate the places of Christ's earthly ministry and passion. These expeditions from the West were called "Crusades," and pious adventurers went with them from all parts of Europe. A man who died upon a crusade thought that he was fairly sure of going straight to Heaven. This first Crusade was successsful and a Christian kingdom was set up in Jerusalem, which lasted there for eighty-eight years, and, in some parts of Palestine, for nearly two hundred years. Europe learned much from the Crusades, and many luxuries, arts and crafts were brought back to it from the East. But the name got much abused,

The first Crusade, 1096.

and at last the Popes called every private quarrel
of their own a crusade, promising their blessing
to all who paid money to it, and scolding all
who refused.

A prudent yet wicked English king like Rufus
stayed at home in spite of the Pope's scoldings,
and grabbed as much as he could of the property
of his neighbours who went upon the Crusade.

Henry I,
1100-1135.
When Robert came back he found that he had
lost another chance. Rufus had been shot in
the year 1100, while hunting in the New Forest,
and his youngest brother, Henry, had seized the
crown of England. Of course Robert rebelled,
and the great barons, both of England and Normandy, with him. But, equally of course,
Henry and his faithful Englishmen made short
work of every rebellion. English chroniclers
called Henry I the "Lion of Justice," and it was
not a bad name for him. Though cruel and
selfish, he was a much more respectable character than Rufus, and he kept order splen-
didly. He was a man of learning, which till
then had been unusual in royal families. "An
unlearned king," he used to say, "is a crowned
ass." Only one of his descendants, before the
eighteenth century, was wholly unlearned, and
that was Edward II, who came to a bad end.
Henry endeared himself to his Englishmen by
marrying the last princess of the old Saxon race,

Edith, daughter of Queen Margaret of Scotland, who was the great-great-granddaughter of Ethelred the Unready. Among Henry's courtiers and servants we often find the names of Englishmen as well as Normans, though all the highest places in the Church were still held by Normans or by men of mixed race. Well able to fight, and quite ready to do so when it was necessary, Henry, like other clever kings, avoided all unnecessary wars, and got on well with the Scottish and sometimes even with the French kings.

But his only son was drowned in the wreck of the *White Ship* in crossing the Channel; and when Henry died, in 1135, his heir was his only daughter, Matilda, whose second husband was Geoffrey Plantagenet, Count of Anjou in France. Now no woman had ever reigned in England, and so, when Count Stephen of Blois, son of William I's daughter Adela, appeared in London and claimed the crown, he was welcomed as King, although he and most of the barons had already promised to uphold the claim of Matilda. Stephen was known to be a kind-hearted fellow who would not rule too strictly; he was in fact just like his uncle Robert. Stephen and Matilda, 1135-54.

Alas for England! Matilda, naturally enough, claimed her "rights," and civil war began almost at once. Nothing could have suited the barons Civil War 1138-52.

better. They changed sides continually and fought now for Stephen and now for Matilda, as long as there was any one left to fight. "For nineteen winters," says the old English chronicler, who was still writing in his monastery at Peterboro, "this went on." Castles sprang up everywhere, "full of devils," who tortured men for their riches, made war for sport, burned towns and corn crops, coined their own money and compelled the poor to take it in payment. At the end of the reign it was said there were over three hundred unlicensed castles in England. Poor Stephen did his best; he flew hither and thither besieging these castles, but seldom had patience to take one. He and Matilda (who was just as bad, and a horrid female into the bargain) could only think of bribing the great barons to fight for them by heaping lands, riches, and offices on them; and, between the pair of them, the treasures of the crown of England were soon spent. The King of Scots, David I, who was Matilda's cousin, rushed in at the very beginning with a great army of wild men, and, though the Yorkshiremen gave him a sound thrashing at the "Battle of the Standard," near Northallerton (1138), he stuck to Cumberland, and Stephen soon tried to bribe him by giving him Northumberland also. So, as the old chronicler says, "it seemed to Eng-

The barons are let loose.

"Battle of the Standard."

lishmen as if God slept and all His saints." The Church alone remained a refuge for the oppressed, and, naturally enough, the Church came out at the end of it all, not only much richer, but with much more power over the hearts of men.

At last, in 1152, young Henry, the son of Matilda and Geoffrey, made peace at Wallingford with Stephen, who was now an old and worn-out man. Henry was to govern England as chief minister while Stephen lived, and then to succeed to the crown. And in two years Stephen died and Henry II became King of England.

Peace made at Wallingford, 1152.

CHAPTER IV

HENRY II TO HENRY III, 1154-1272: THE BEGINNINGS OF PARLIAMENT

The task of the King in 1154. THE young man of twenty-one whom we call Henry II came to a country absolutely wasted with civil war. When he died, thirty-five years later, he left it the richest, the most peaceful, the most intelligent, and most united kingdom in Europe. There is no misery like that of civil war; there have been two civil wars since that date, one in the fifteenth and one in the seventeenth century; and of course during these wars the country people suffered. But so firmly did the sense of law and order, which Henry II drove into his people's heads, take root, that there was no complete upset of civil life, even in these later civil wars. We cannot of course attribute all the later good fortune of the country to one man, not even to such a great and wise man as Henry II. His path had been prepared for him long before, and he was extraordinarily fortunate in his opportunity.

A great revival of intelligence had already begun all over Europe, and a great revival of
trade, no doubt largely owing to the lessons
learned in the Crusades.   Long-neglected books
of Roman Law had been found, and French
and Italian lawyers were reading them.   Schools
were increasing, and even "universities," of
which Oxford was the first in England, were
beginning.   The towns had been gaining in
riches in spite of the civil war; London, to which
Henry I had given a "charter," allowing it to
govern itself and keep its own customs, was
even more ahead of the other English towns
than it is to-day.   The difference of race between Norman and Englishman was being forgotten.   We were growing into one "people."
The worst followers of the worst barons had
killed each other off during the war, or gone
away to the Crusades.   Henry had little
difficulty in getting rid of those that remained,
and knocking down their ramshackle castles.

His fa-
vourable
opportu-
nity.

But great as the opportunity was, it would
have been of no use if Henry had not been a very
great man; one of the greatest kings who ever
lived.   His power of work, and of making other
people work, was amazing; he seemed to have
a hundred pairs of eyes.   Laziness was to him
the one unpardonable crime.   For pomp, even
for dignity, he cared nothing.   He was cursed,

Charac-
ter of
Henry II.

as all kings of his race were, with the most frightful temper; but he was merciful and forgiving when his rage was over. Norman on the mother's side, English on the grandmother's, he was the most French of Frenchmen by his father's family, the House of Anjou. He had just married Eleanor of Aquitaine, the greatest heiress in Europe, who owned all Southwestern France, from the River Loire to the Pyrenees.

His foreign possessions really a burden to him.

Aquitaine, or "Gascony," or "Guienne," as the southern part of it is called, was a land of small and very turbulent nobles, who could never get enough fighting. Even Henry never succeeded in keeping them in order. But of course, with all this land, and with the riches of England at his back, Henry ought to have been a much more powerful man than his "overlord," the King of France. Yet the truth is that all these different French provinces, — Normandy, Anjou, Maine, Touraine, Aquitaine—were rather a trouble than an advantage to him. They cost more to keep in order than they brought

Hostility of England and France.

in in rents and taxes, and they led to continual quarrels, mostly about frontier castles, with the French King Louis VII and his successor, Philip II. Henry and his son, Richard I, in fact did well in keeping their huge loosely knit bundle of provinces together as long as they

did. John, who succeeded Richard, lost all
the best parts of them at once.

For the kings of France were doing just what
our kings were doing; they were trying to make
all Frenchmen feel that they were one people.
So Henry, Richard, and John were really fighting
a losing battle in France. For the details of
that battle I do not care two straws. Moreover,
our sympathies *ought* to be on the side of the
French kings, unless they invaded England.

What really matters to us is what Henry was
doing in England. You may be sure that he
gave no one any rest there, neither his many
friends, nor his few foes. The greatest thing
England owes to him is the system of Law,
which really began in his reign, and has gone
on being improved by skilful lawyers ever
since. Till his reign, all the King's servants,
sheriffs, officers, bishops, and the rest had acted
as judges, rent collectors, soldiers, taxing-men
without distinction; and the King's courts
of justice had been held wherever the King
happened to be. But Henry picked out specially trained men for judges, and confined them
to the one business of judging. He chose men
who knew some Roman Law, and who would be
able to improve our stupid, old-fashioned customs by its light. He swept away a great
many of such customs, among other things the

Henry II as Law-giver.

fines for murder, which he treated by hanging; he built prisons in every county, and kept offenders in them until the judges came round "on circuit," as, you know, they still do four times a year. The judges gave these offenders a fair trial, in which some sort of "jury" of their neighbours had a hand; and if they were found guilty they were hanged — which surprised them a good deal. The King could not wholly put down the barons' private courts of justice, but he took away every shred of real power from them; his sheriffs, he said, were to go *everywhere*, no matter what privileges a baron might claim. Another splendid thing which Henry did was to establish one coinage for the whole country, stamped at his royal mint; and woe it was to the man who "uttered" false coins!

He trains the nation to war.
As regards his army of freeholders, he compelled every man to keep arms in his house, to be used when the sheriff called him to battle. A rich landowner had to be armed in complete chain mail, to provide his own horses and to serve in the cavalry, and was called a "knight." But even a man who possessed the small sum of £6 13s. 4d. had to provide himself with a steel cap, a neck-piece of mail, and a spear; while every free man, in town or country, had to have a leather jacket, a steel cap, and a spear. And this "territorial army" was not only to

fight, but to keep the peace also, to chase rogues and thieves, to watch at night at the town gates; in fact, as we should now say, to "assist the police."

As regards taxes, Henry did not demand huge sums from all his subjects without distinction of wealth, but he sent officials round the country, who called together the principal inhabitants of each village and town, and got them to say what their neighbours as well as themselves could afford to pay. So you see, by all these measures, King Henry *interested his subjects in the government.* He made them see that they had duties as well as rights, a fact which the poorer classes of Englishmen have almost wholly forgotten to-day. *His taxes.*

But for one frightful stroke of ill-luck Henry might have left an England completely united. Hear the story of St. Thomas Becket. *His quarrel with Thomas Becket, 1164-70.*

The twelfth century was the "golden age" of the Church. The aims of the popes, even of those popes who were most hostile to the growth of nations, were not entirely selfish. Christendom was to them one family which God had given them to rule. Kings were to be the earthly instruments of their will, to be petted as long as they obeyed, but scolded and even deposed when they did not. No king and no lay court of justice was to dare to touch a priest, much less to hang him if he committed murder or theft, which too many priests still did. Henry wanted to hang such priests. He was told of a hundred murders committed by priests in the first ten years of his reign which had gone unpunished, because the Church said all priests were "sacred." So he chose his favourite minister, Thomas Becket, already Chancellor of England, to be Archbishop of Canterbury. He believed that Thomas would help him to make one law for clergymen and laymen alike; but Thomas, as proud and hot-tempered a man as the King, had no sooner become Archbishop than he turned right round and supported the most extreme claims of the Church. He even went farther than the Pope, who was most anxious not to quarrel with Henry. "The Church lands," he said, "should pay no taxes; as for hanging priests, he would not hear of it." Henry was naturally furious, especially when Thomas went abroad and stirred up the King of France and the Pope against him. After a long and weary quarrel Henry, in a fit of passion, used some rash words which some wicked courtiers interpreted to mean that they were to kill Thomas. They slipped away secretly from the King's court and murdered the Archbishop in his own cathedral.

Such a deed of horror was unknown since the

Murder of Becket, 1170.

·THE MURDER OF BECKET·

days of the heathen Danes. Thomas at once became both martyr and saint, even in the eyes of those who had hated his pride while he lived. Men believed that miracles were worked at his tomb, that a touch of his bones would restore the dead to life. A pilgrimage to his shrine at Canterbury became before long the duty of every pious Englishman.

"Saint Thomas the Martyr."

But the worst result was that all the King's attempts to bring the Churchmen under the law utterly failed; and the claims of the Church to be independent of the State actually increased for a century to come. All Henry's enemies also took the opportunity to jump on him at once. A fearful outbreak of the barons (who had been quiet for twenty years), both in England and Normandy, came to a head in 1174, and was supported by both the French and Scottish kings, by Henry's own eldest son (a vain young fool), and by Queen Eleanor herself. Henry's throne rocked and tottered; but, of course, all good Englishmen stood stiffly for their King, and, when he had knelt in penitence at Becket's tomb, and allowed the Canterbury monks to give him a sound flogging there, he triumphed over his enemies. He took the King of Scots prisoner, and compelled the rest of the barons to sue for mercy. This mercy he freely gave them. No one was hanged for the

The last baronial rebellion, 1174-5.

rebellion, and most people concerned got off with a fine.

Henry II's later years, 1175-89.

His last six years were again disturbed by revolts, but not in England. Philip II was the first of the really great French kings bent on uniting all Frenchmen; and he easily enticed, not only Henry's barons, but his three younger sons, Richard, Geoffrey and John, into rebellion. Henry died of a broken heart at their ingratitude in 1189.

His visit to Ireland 1171-2.

One event of his reign must not be forgotten, his visit to Ireland in 1171-2. St. Patrick, you may have heard, had banished the snakes from that island, but had not succeeded in banishing the murderers and thieves, who were worse than many snakes. In spite of some few settlements

State of Ireland.

of Danish pirates and traders on the eastern coast, Ireland had remained purely Celtic and purely a pasture country. All wealth was reck, oned in cows; Rome had never set foot there, so there was a king for every day in the week, and the sole amusement of such persons was to drive off each other's cows, and to kill all who resisted. In Henry II's time this had been going on for at least 700 years, and during the 700 that have followed much the same thing would have been going on if the English government had not occasionally interfered.

Well, in 1168, one of these wild kings, being

in more than usual trouble, came to Henry and asked for help. Henry said, "Oh, go and try some of my barons on the Welsh border; they are fine fighting-men. I have no objection to their going to help you." The Welsh border barons promptly went, and, of course, being well armed and trained, a few hundred of their soldiers simply drove everything before them in Ireland, and won, as their reward, enormous estates there. The King began to be anxious about the business, and so, in 1171, he sailed over to Waterford and spent half a year in Ireland. The Irish kings hastened, one after another, to make complete submission to him; he confirmed his English subjects in their new possessions; he divided the island into counties, appointed sheriffs and judges for it — and then he went home. He had made only a half-conquest, which is always a bad business, and the English he left behind him soon became as wild and barbarous as the Irishmen themselves.

Henry was succeeded in all his vast dominions by his eldest surviving son, Richard I, "Richard the Lion Heart," "Richard Yea and Nay," so called because he spoke the truth. He found England at profound peace; his father's great lawyers and ministers continued to govern it for him until his death ten years later. He himself cared little for it, except for the money

Richard I. 1189-99.

he could squeeze out of it to serve the two objects which really interested him. These were to deliver Jerusalem, which had again been taken by the Saracens, and to save his foreign provinces from being swallowed by the French King.

Richard on the Crusade; his quarrels with France.

Richard was a most gallant soldier and a born leader of men in war; he was generous and forgiving; but of his father's really great qualities he had very few. He had been spoiled as a child, and he remained a great, jolly, impatient child till his death. He and his rival, King Philip, at once set out on the Crusade in 1190, and quarrelled continually. Philip soon slipped off home, and began to grab Richard's French provinces, with the aid of the treacherous John, Richard's youngest brother, who had stayed in England. John was the one unmitigated scoundrel in the whole family; and he rejoiced greatly when he heard that his brother, who had failed to deliver Jerusalem, had been taken captive on his way home from Palestine, by the unscrupulous German Emperor, Henry VI. This royal brigand demanded an enormous ransom for Richard, and of course heavy taxes had to be raised in England to pay him. But it did not interrupt the good peace, and Richard, who forgave his wicked brother directly he was free, spent the rest of his short reign in France fighting King Philip, not altogether without success. He was killed at the siege of a small French castle in 1199.

The proper heir to the throne was Arthur of Brittany, a mere boy, son of Henry II's third son Geoffrey, who had died in 1186. But John was in England and seized the crown without much difficulty. Of course he quarrelled at once with his old friend Philip, and Philip knew that his own time and that of France had now come. John did, indeed, get hold of little Arthur and had him murdered; but then dawdled away his time in small sieges and useless raids in France, while Philip overran all John's French dominions except Aquitaine with perfect ease.

John, 1199-1216.

Murder of Prince Arthur, about 1203.

By 1205, Normandy, Maine, Touraine, Anjou, the inheritance of the mighty Norman and Angevin races, had gone to France for good. And of the French possessions of England only the far South-west remained.

Loss of Normandy, 1205.

The English barons, most of whom had owned lands in Normandy ever since 1066, were of course furious with their King, especially when he kept on screwing enormous sums of money from them, calling out large armies to fight, and then running away without fighting. As for Aquitaine, none of them owned lands there, and they refused to defend it. John raved and cursed, and practised horrible cruelties on any

Anger of the barons.

enemies he could catch, and generally behaved in a most unkingly fashion. But in 1206 he began quite a new quarrel with the English Church and the Pope. His cause was at first a good one, for it was about the appointment of the Archbishop of Canterbury. Both the Pope and the monks at Canterbury had refused to accept the man whom John named as Archbishop; and the Pope had even appointed one Stephen Langton in his place. John swore "by God's teeth" that he would never receive Langton as Archbishop; and for five years he held his own. The Pope tried every weapon at his command; he "excommunicated" John, that is to say, he cut him off from all Christian rites; he put England under an "interdict," which meant that no one could be buried with the full burial service, no one married in church, no church bells rung, and in fact all the best religious services and sacraments were suspended. Finally, the Pope declared John deposed and told Philip to go and depose him.

John's quarrel with Pope Innocent III, 1206-13.

Now, much as Englishmen hated their tyrannical King, they hated still more the idea of an Italian priest dealing thus with the crown and liberty of England; and most honest men were prepared to support even John against Philip and the Pope.

John, for his part, confiscated all Church

property in England and bestowed it on a set of foreign favourites and parasites, mostly mercenary soldiers from Flanders. Then suddenly he gave away his own cause. In 1213 he became frightened, made the most abject submission to the Pope, and promised to hold his crown and country for the future as the Pope's "vassal," and to pay tribute for it. This was too much for all Englishmen, and the country fairly boiled over with rage. *John submits to the Pope, 1213.* *Fury of Englishmen.*

Yet "rebellion" was a dreadful thing. John was rich, powerful, and held all the important castles of England in his own hands. The man who gave the English barons courage to resist was the very man over whom all this fuss had begun — Stephen Langton. He called meetings of the leading barons, and either drew up or got them to draw up a list of their grievances and those of other classes of Englishmen. This document was to be taken to the King and, if he refused to listen, the barons were to rebel. Nearly all the towns and most of the churchmen were on their side; yet they were only able to raise a little army of 2,000 men. Luckily John again lost his head and agreed to all their demands. The document which they presented to him at Runnymede, near Windsor, in June, 1215, and which he signed, was called "Magna Charta" — the "Great Charter of Liberties." *The barons lead the revolt of the Nation, 1214, 1215.* *The Great Charter of 1215.*

John soon repented of signing it, sent for his hireling soldiers, sent to his "Holy Father," the Pope (who at once absolved him from his oath to observe the Charter, and hurled dreadful curses at the rebel barons), and scattered the little national army like chaff before him. In despair some of the barons took the foolish step of calling in Prince Louis of France and offering him the English crown. But within fifteen months England was saved. John, having grossly overeaten himself one night at Newark Abbey, died suddenly in October, 1216.

Death of John, 1216.

Contents of the Great Charter.

If you will consider the Great Charter for a few minutes you will see what a long road toward union and peace England had travelled since the last barons' rebellion in 1174. In that year the fight had been one of barons against King and people; now it was one of barons and people against King. All classes of the nation suffered and had called on the barons to lead them. They could not have done this if the barons had still held their lands in Normandy; and so it was the loss of those lands that finally made the barons Englishmen.

The nation had grown up; it had "come of age." What it wanted was to make its King give security that he would not oppress it in future. So, by the Great Charter, it proposed

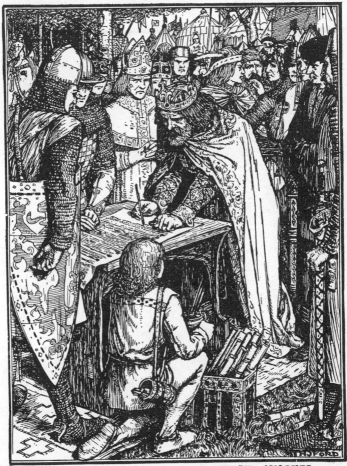

KING JOHN SIGNS THE GREAT CHARTER

to "tie his hands" in several ways.   He is not to
levy any more land-taxes without calling his
Great Council of all the great landowners
(barons and others), and asking their consent.
He is not to exact higher payments of rent or of
other customary dues than earlier kings did.
He is to pay his debts to his creditors.   His
courts of justice shall sit regularly as those of
Henry II and Richard had sat; and they shall
sit in a fixed place instead of rambling over
England and France in the train of the King.
(This "fixed place" came to be Westminster.)
All men shall be entitled to a fair trial, and shall
not be deprived of their land without a fair
trial.   The great abuses of the game laws shall
be abolished.

And so on.   No doubt to many of the barons
of this year, 1215, it was their own grievances
of which they were thinking most — the grind-
ing taxes, the loss of their Norman lands, their
cruelly murdered kinsfolk.   But in order to
get these grievances redressed they were obliged
to ask also for the redress of the grievances from
which other classes were suffering; even "villeins"
are carefully protected by one of the articles of
the Charter; even to the hated Scots and Welsh
"justice" is to be done.   To the Church much
more than justice is to be done; it is to be "made
free," which, I fear, means that the kings are

not to appoint its bishops. But later kings
always found a way of avoiding this restric-
tion.

THE REEDS OF RUNNYMEDE

Runny-
mede,
June 15,
1215.

At Runnymede, at Runnymede,
    What say the reeds at Runnymede?
The lissom reeds that give and take,
That bend so far, but never break,
They keep the sleepy Thames awake
    With tales of John at Runnymede.

At Runnymede, at Runnymede,
    Oh hear the reeds at Runnymede:
"You mustn't sell, delay, deny,
A freeman's right or liberty,
It wakes the stubborn Englishry,
    We saw 'em roused at Runnymede!

"When through our ranks the Barons came,
With little thought of praise or blame,
But resolute to play the game,
    They lumbered up to Runnymede;
And there they launched in solid line,
The first attack on Right Divine —
The curt, uncompromising 'Sign!'
    That settled John at Runnymede.

"At Runnymede, at Runnymede,
Your rights were won at Runnymede!
No freeman shall be fined or bound,
  Or dispossessed of freehold ground,
  Except by lawful judgment found
  And passed upon him by his peers!—
Forget not, after all these years,
  The Charter signed at Runnymede."

And still when mob or monarch lays
Too rude a hand on English ways,
The whisper wakes, the shudder plays,
  Across the reeds at Runnymede.
And Thames, that knows the moods of kings,
And crowds and priests and suchlike things,
Rolls deep and dreadful as he brings
  Their warning down from Runnymede!

John's heir was a boy of nine years, who was **Henry III, 1216-72.** to reign for fifty-six years as Henry III. A wise Regent was quickly chosen for him, William Marshall, Earl of Pembroke; the French prince was still in the land, but his friends soon deserted him, and he was glad to make a treaty and go away. The Pope supported the new **The power of the Pope.** government, for by John's submission the young King had become his "vassal." The Pope expected to make a good thing out of it, and he intended Henry to help him, which

Henry, when he grew up, was only too ready to
do. For the King, with many good qualities,
such as piety and mercy, with much learning
and good taste for art and building, was quite
un-English. He was the first king, since Edward the Confessor, who had leaned wholly
upon foreign favourites and despised his own
sturdy people. He was frightfully extravagant,
and a natural, though not an intentional, liar.
England was to him only a very rich farm, out of
which he could squeeze for himself and the " Holy
Father," the Pope at Rome, cash, more cash,
and ever more and more cash. His own share
of it he spent on building beautiful churches,
such as Westminster Abbey, and in useless
wars with his noble overlord, King Louis IX of
France, who always beat him, but allowed him
to retain Southern Aquitaine, that is, Gascony.
Down till about 1232 Henry governed by native
English or Norman ministers; and, so long as
Langton lived, the Pope did not interfere much.
But soon after that the King's extravagance and
the Pope's increasing demands for money began
to be felt, and the nation grumbled. The
barons were now thorough Englishmen, who
had no interests outside England at all. They
began to wonder whether Magna Charta was
a mere bit of waste paper or not; the King
observed few of its provisions, though he con-

stantly swore to observe them. In fact, he published it at the beginning of his reign with several important articles omitted. Yet it was difficult to catch him out. He was not in the least a "gory tyrant," like his father; he simply maddened every one by his useless extravagances, by never paying his debts, and by never keeping his promises. At last the barons found that he had promised the Pope an enormous sum of money, in return for which the Pope had promised to one of Henry's sons the crown of Sicily. Sicily, forsooth! What had England to do with an island in the Mediterranean, while French pirates were burning the towns on our south coast without a single King's ship being sent to prevent them?

Remonstrance of the barons.

This was in 1257. The barons met the King in council after council and utterly refused to pay a penny for the Sicilian job. Endless documents were drawn up for the King to sign. He signed them quite readily, promised whatever he was asked, but never kept his word. The chief spokesman of the barons was one Simon de Montfort, Earl of Leicester. The nation and all the best of the churchmen rallied heartily to Simon's side, especially the men of London, and things ended in a kind of war, wherein, at the battle of Lewes in 1264, the King and his eldest son, Prince Edward, fell

National rising, 1257-65.

Simon de Montfort.

into Earl Simon's hands. For a year Simon governed in the King's name; but he was a hot-headed and rather grasping man, and quarrelled with his own best supporters. He even

Prince Edward learns a lesson.

called in the aid of the Welsh. At last Prince Edward escaped from captivity, rallied his father's friends, defeated and slew Simon at Evesham, and put his father back on the throne. Little vengeance was taken; and the last seven years of Henry's reign were peaceful, so peaceful indeed, that, though Prince Edward was away in Palestine when Henry died in 1272, no one questioned his right to be crowned king when he returned.

The Friars in England.

Two things rendered Henry's long reign memorable; the coming of the Friars, and the beginning of Parliament. The Friars were the last offshoot of the dying tree of monkery. Wise people began to see that a monk who shut himself up in a monastery might no doubt save his own soul, but could do little for the souls of other people. What was wanted was men who could go about *in the world* preaching and doing good. Two great men, St. Dominic, a Spaniard, and St. Francis, an Italian, founded brotherhoods of "Friars" (the word means brothers), who were to fulfil this mission. It was a splendid idea, and St. Francis is one of the most beautiful figures in history. The Friars came and lodged with the very poor in the filthy slums, and did such work as our clergy are doing to-day in all great cities. Others walked all over the land, preaching in the streets and villages. But soon this movement also began to fail; for pious laymen heaped lands and riches on these brotherhoods, until in little more than a century they had become as rich and as worldly as the monks. Moreover, the ordinary parish and town priests, who suffered even more than the laymen from the greedy demands of the Pope, began to think of monks and friars alike, as mere agents of the Pope, as something foreign to the "national Church." Hence, after 1300, there were few gifts of land to monks or friars; people preferred rather, to found schools and colleges. Both at Oxford and Cambridge colleges had been founded before that year. Schools and colleges.

The second thing, the beginning of Parliament, is even more important. Ever since Magna Charta had been signed the idea that the nation ought in some way to control the King was in the air; and the question was what shape this control should take. As you know, Parliament to-day consists of two houses, Lords and Commons. The House of Lords is a direct descendant of the barons of the thirteenth century. The eldest son of a baron, The Germ of Parliament. The House of Lords.

earl, marquis, or duke inherits the right to receive from the King a letter calling him by name to Parliament whenever it meets. The King can "create" a man a baron, and the creation carries with it this right to receive the letter of summons. Perhaps there were nearly two hundred great barons in Henry III's reign; there are now over six hundred. The bishops always received a similar letter of summons, and, until the Reformation, so did the leading abbots. It was in the reign of Henry III that this Great Council began to take its shape. The King no doubt disliked it, for he disliked all control, and its business certainly was to control him. But he found that he could not do without it.

The House of Commons. The origin of the House of Commons is quite different. It, to-day, also has over six hundred members, chosen from different towns and districts of the United Kingdom, by all persons who have the right to vote. Now, in the reign of Henry III, and even earlier, as I told you, the King had been in the habit of sending officials into each county and town to consult with the chief landowners and citizens, and to discover what amount of taxes that county or city could bear. These people met in the old Saxon court of justice, called the "County Court," to which all free landowners ought to come; and they elected "knights" or gentlemen to speak for them. In Henry III's reign the brilliant idea occurred to somebody, "Why not send these elected knights or gentlemen to meet the King himself in some general assembly? Each of them can speak for his own county, and the King will get a fair idea of what amount of money the whole of England is able to give him."

Now no general assembly other than that of the Great Council of barons existed, so the elected knights from the counties and the elected citizens from the towns used occasionally to be called to the Great Council, and there met the barons and the King. Then there would be a great Talking or "Parliamentum" (French *parler*, to talk). Such knights and citizens would naturally grow bolder when they found themselves met together, and found that the barons were much the same sort of fellows as themselves, and had the same ideas about the King's extravagance and his ridiculous foreign wars. It was on such occasions that they thoroughly realized that the barons were their natural leaders. Soon, they too would begin to present petitions about the grievances of their districts, and to beg the King to make particular laws. Earl Simon has got much fame because, while he was ruling in 1265, there met, for the first time, in one assembly,

The first Parliaments in the reign of Henry III.

barons, bishops, abbots, "knights of the shire," and citizens. You will see in the next chapter how Edward I shaped these assemblies into regular parliaments, and what powers they won for themselves.

My Father's Chair.

There are four good legs to my Father's
    Chair —
  Priest and People and Lords and Crown.
I sit on all of 'em fair and square,
  And that is the reason it don't break down.

I won't trust one leg, nor two, nor three,
  To carry my weight when I sit me down;
I want all four of 'em under me —
  Priest and People and Lords and Crown.

I sit on all four and I favour none —
  Priest, nor People, nor Lords, nor Crown —
And I never tilt in my Chair, my son,
  And that is the reason it don't break down!

When your time comes to sit in my Chair,
  Remember your Father's habits and rules:
Sit on all four legs, fair and square,
  And never be tempted by one-legged stools!

CHAPTER V

THE THREE EDWARDS, 1272—1377

EDWARD I, II, and III (notice the grand old Saxon name; we are all one people now) may be called Edward the Lawgiver, Edward the Poltroon, Edward the Knight. The greatest of these was Edward I.

He ranks with the half dozen greatest "makers of England," with Alfred, William the Conqueror, Henry II, Henry VIII, Elizabeth, and Victoria the Great. I should, indeed, say "makers of Britain," for it was Edward who planned, and almost carried out, the union of the whole island under one crown. It was he who gave the abiding shape to our Parliament, who dealt the first successful blow to the pretensions of the Pope, and who first armed his soldiers with the all-conquering longbow. His care for our coast defences was an example to his descendants. His legal reforms were hardly less than those of Henry II, and at the end of his reign the law of England and the law courts of England had

Edward I, 1272-1307.

taken the shape that they bore down to the nineteenth century.

His charac-ter,

Edward I was a brave, truthful, honourable man, of rather narrow sympathies, and could be very cruel to his foes. He had learned much from his father's muddled reign; he would engage in no rash foreign adventures to please the Pope or any one else. Of course, he must defend his one foreign possession, Gascony; and he fortified it very strongly. Occasionally he was obliged to fight King Philip IV of France, but that was because that cunning gentleman was trying to swallow not only Gascony but also little Flanders, which was now the most important market for English wool, and also because Philip was helping Edward's enemies the Scots. What Edward himself was really set upon was the union of Wales and Scotland to England. With Wales he was finally successful. After two or three long and patient campaigns, full of painful marches and costly castle-building, he managed to shut up Llewellyn, the last "Prince of North Wales," in the mountainous district of Snowdon; and when Llewellyn was killed in a skirmish, Edward organized Wales into counties, with regular sheriffs, judges and law courts, all under the English crown. From that time the eldest son of the King of England has

and his task.

Conquest of Wales, 1282.

~ EDWARD I.'S WARS WITH THE WELSH ~
How the King shared the hardships of his men

always borne the name of "Prince of Wales."
The first Englishman to be Prince of Wales
could at least speak no English when the title
was given to him, for he was only a few hours
old. But the King stained his victory by the
cruel execution of a Welsh prince, David, who,
after all, had only done what all Celtic princes
had been doing for centuries, namely, promised
to submit and then rebelled again.

With Scotland Edward just failed, and his
failure brought a terrible retribution on both
countries. For nearly a century before this
time Scotland had been at peace with England, and its southern half had been growing richer and happier. Many Norman and
English barons owned lands on both sides of
the border and so were "vassals" of the kings
of both countries. Even the Scottish King
held a small English earldom, and for that he
was, of course, the "vassal" of King Edward.
But the crown of Scotland he held from God
alone, as Edward held the crown of England.

King Alexander III of Scotland died in 1286,
leaving an infant grand-daughter known as the
"Maid of Norway." Edward at once proposed to marry her to his eldest son. Nothing
could have been better for both kingdoms, and
all reasonable Scots would have welcomed a
union. But in 1290 the baby queen died, and

Attempt
to con-
quer
Scotland,
1294-
1307.

Pros-
perity of
Scotland
before
Edward
I's wars.

Contest
for the
Scottish
crown,
1290.

at once there was a dispute for the crown
between several great Scottish barons. They
appealed to Edward, and in their appeal acknowledged him to be "overlord" of Scotland.
He gave his decision in favour of John Balliol,
who was duly crowned at Scone as King of
Scotland.

Edward's
attack on
Scotland,
1294.

Then, in his new capacity as overlord,
Edward began to bully Balliol and to treat
Scotland as if it were already a part of England.
Balliol was a weak creature, and threw himself into the arms of Philip of France, who saw
a splendid opportunity of diverting Edward
from Flanders and Gascony by aiding the
Scots. So was founded the great alliance
between France and Scotland which was to
last for over two hundred years. Edward
thereon declared Balliol deposed and sent men
to conquer Scotland. He only succeeded in
rousing every Scottish heart to desperate

William
Wallace.

resistance. Of this resistance a small landowner, called William Wallace, was the first
hero. Edward, with his mailed knights and
his terrible archers, gave Wallace and the
Scots a severe thrashing at Falkirk (1298), but
he could not hunt down a whole nation in that
wild hill country. During the nine years
between the battle of Falkirk and Edward's
death it became a war to the knife between the

two nations, which ten years before had been ready to lie down like lambs together.

The result was that, for fifty miles on each side of the border, the land became a desert, through which swept, almost yearly, fierce raids from either country; and this state of things continued far into the sixteenth century. Every Scot whom Edward caught he would hang as a traitor (Wallace was hanged in 1305), which was quite a new practice in foreign or even in civil war, wherein there had been a great deal of "live and let live" on either side. Like other narrow and upright men, Edward failed to see that those who resisted him could be as upright as himself. Yet he was such a good soldier and so patient that he had very nearly finished off the conquest of all Southern Scotland when he died on his last campaign in 1307. "Carry my bones into battle against them," were his last instructions, "and on my tomb carve 'Edward, the hammer of the Scots.'" But it was too late; Scotland had just found a deliverer in Robert Bruce, a baron of Norman descent, who was crowned at Scone in 1306 as King Robert I.

The "Border" and the Border-wars, 1300-1550

Robert Bruce, King of Scotland, 1306.

Great as a warrior and imperialist, Edward was even greater as a lawgiver and organizer. All his laws obtained the full sanction of the now regularly constituted House of Lords.

Edward I's Parliaments.

The House of Commons generally met at the same time, and was made up of over two hundred borough-members and seventy-four Knights of the Shire. It had, at first, no share in the *law-making*, but it constantly petitioned in favour of particular laws. The clergy, after a short struggle, preferred not to be represented in Parliament except by their bishops and great abbots, who sat with the Lords; but Edward allowed them two assemblies called "Convocations," one in the Archbishopric of Canterbury and one in that of York. These bodies voted taxes for the clergy to pay, just as Lords and Commons voted them for the laymen to pay.

His Lawgiving.

The House of Lords also became the chief law court to which you could "appeal" from all the three "common" law courts, which were now fixed at Westminster, with a separate staff of judges for each. In some cases, if you couldn't get justice anywhere else, you might go to the King himself, who would order his Chancellor to look into your case; and that was the beginning of the "Court of Chancery." The Chancellor was the greatest official in the kingdom and kept the King's "Great Seal," with which all legal documents must be sealed. One of the most useful laws which Edward made was called

"Mortmain," forbidding people to leave more lands to the Church, which was growing a little too powerful. Another was the "Statute of Winchester," a great measure for compelling all men to help in keeping the peace; it created "police-constables" (with whom, as friends or foes, most boys are still familiar) in every town and village. Another was a law allowing the free sale and division of great estates of land. In all his laws, as in all his wars, we may say that Edward, like Henry II, *took his people into his confidence*, which is the secret of good government. It was expensive, as all good government must be; and, as no one likes paying taxes, there was once a sort of outbreak, both of barons and clergy, against the expense of it. Edward was very angry, but he gave way and confirmed Magna Charta, with the additional promise added that he would take no taxes at all without consent of his full Parliament.

His heavy taxes.

He kept his promise. "Pactum serva" (keep troth) was his motto. Indeed the country was now able to bear heavy taxes. Early in the twelfth century an order of monks called "Cistercians" had begun to devote themselves to breeding sheep on a great scale, in order to sell wool; and England at the end of the thirteenth century was the greatest wool-growing country in the world. We did

Riches of England; growth of wool.

not yet know how to weave fine cloth, so our
wool was all exported to Flanders, and Parliament said that every sack that was sent there
should pay the King 6s. 8d. The "Flemings"
(men of Flanders) wove the cloth and sent it
all over Europe. This trade made it more
important than ever for our kings to keep the
sea clear of pirates, and Edward worked hard
at this task. There were other rich trades
such as that in wine with Bordeaux, and in
furs and leather with North Germany; foreign
merchants had to pay the King something for
leave to come to sell and buy, for as yet there
were very few English merchant-ships.

Edward I's quarrel with the clergy was a
very short and simple affair. The English
Church had been long growing more and more
a part of the nation and less and less dependent
on the Pope. But still the Pope was the head
of all European churches, and had to be obeyed
if possible. In 1296 Pope Boniface VIII
startled the whole of Europe by absolutely
forbidding any clergyman to pay any taxes
to any king. It was only a few years since
Edward had got his regular system of taxing
the clergy comfortably arranged. He and the
King of France rose in wrath against this
absurd suggestion. Edward simply told his
clergy that he would put them "out of law"

(*i.e.*, withdraw all legal protection from them) if they obeyed the Pope; and he seized all their wool by way of precaution. They very soon gave way. The King of France went much further; he sent men to Italy who maltreated the haughty Pope and the Pope died, perhaps in consequence of the rough handling he got. He put a creature of his own on the Papal throne, and compelled him to come and live in France. For seventy years this "Captivity" of Popes lasted (1305-78), and, as England was at war with France for much of that time, the respect of Englishmen for a French Pope was naturally slight. After the "Captivity" came the "Schism" (division) (1378–1415), during which there were two and sometimes three persons each calling himself Pope. In fact the old Church of the Middle Ages was fast going down hill.

The decay of the Popes, 1300-1500.

Edward's death closes the best period of these "Middle Ages." From that time to the Reformation the country, except in material wealth, did not improve. Even the glorious foreign wars of Edward III brought in the long run more harm than good to England.

Death of Edward I, 1307.

Edward II ("the Poltroon") was a most impossible person, heartless, ignorant, extravagant, cruel, and weak-minded. Men rubbed their eyes and said, "Is this creature the son

Edward II, 1307-27.

His idle-
ness and
extrava-
gance.

The Earl
of Lan-
caster.

Decay of
the
baronage,
1300-
1500.

Deposi-
tion of
Edward
II, 1327.

of 'Pactum serva'?" He gave up the Scottish war at once, and, when in 1314 he was obliged to take it up again, his enormous army got a most thorough thrashing from the Scottish spearmen at Bannockburn. He hung on the neck of a low-class Gascon favourite, who made fun of the sober English barons till they caught and killed him. Edward afterward took a fearful revenge on such barons as he could catch, especially on his cousin Earl Thomas of Lancaster. Thus began a feud between the Crown and this man's family which ended in the overthrow of Edward's great-grandson Richard II and eventually in the civil "Wars of the Roses."

The barons grew worse as well as the King —for no one class in a country can be bad without the others suffering; they used the meetings of Parliament to carry on their quarrels. Several of them were of royal descent (from younger sons of Henry III and Edward I); these had married great English heiresses, and began to fight each other for lands and earldoms. The King seemed to be at their mercy. At last, in 1327, a general rising, headed by the wicked French wife of Edward, swept him away and set up his son, aged 13, as Edward III. Edward II was a bad King; but his deposition and murder were a bad job, because there had been no one great national grievance, only a lot of private ones of certain great nobles. He had wasted his life, and in the end was deposed for nothing in particular.

Edward III ("the Knight"), by interesting these barons in his French and Scottish wars, where there were lands and money as well as glory to be gained, snuffed out their quarrels for nearly fifty years; but he, too, had several younger sons who quarrelled with each other after his strong hand was gone. _{Edward III, 1327-77.}

He was a man of many different sides of character. He loved pageants and splendour, but he also loved hard knocks in hard fights by sea and land. He was merchant-king, sailor-king, soldier-king, and Parliament's king too, for he added greatly to the power of the House of Commons, which, when he died, had obtained a full share in all law-making, could call the King's ministers to account if it thought they were misbehaving, and, in fact, was almost as powerful as the House of Lords. It was always ready to vote Edward enormous sums of money. Finally, Edward thoroughly understood the needs of English trade, and he founded English manufactures; for it was he who invited Flemings to come from Flanders and settle in Norwich and teach us how to weave fine cloth. _{His character and popularity.}

The great
French
war called
the Hundred
Years'
War,
1338-
1453.

Causes of
the war.

Edward
claims to
be King of
France,
1340.

Yet Edward has a bad name in history because he plunged England into that great war with France which lasted off and on for 100 years. In the beginning, I think, he could hardly help fighting. At the best of times England and France were rather like two fierce, well-fed dogs, the doors of whose kennels looked right into each other. Edward had wisely begun his reign with several serious attempts to conquer Scotland, and had won a great battle at Halidon Hill in Berwickshire, while, all the time, French help was being poured into Scotland. Then, again, the French never ceased their attempts to eat up our old ally, Flanders, now more than ever necessary to English trade. Finally, no English King of any spirit could refuse to defend Gascony, our one foreign possession. The war opened with a great English victory on the seas, at Sluys off the River Scheldt (1340); and, just before this victory, Edward had been persuaded by the Flemings to come to their help on land and to take the title of "King of France." By English law his claim to the French crown would have been a good one, because his mother was the daughter of King Philip IV, but French law did not recognize that a man could inherit a kingdom through his mother. However, from this time forward

Boundary of Henry II's possessions
English possessions at accession of Edward III
English possessions after Treaty of Bretigny

Calais

FLANDERS

Agincourt

Crecy

R. Scheldt

English Channel

Dieppe

Cherbourg   Havre   Harfleur

Caen   Rouen

NORMANDY

×Tenchebray

BRITTANY   MAINE   Paris

GERMANY

Angers

Orleans

R. Seine

R. Loire

ATLANTIC OCEAN

A
N
J
O
U

T
O
U
R
A
I
N
E

A
Q
U
I
T
A
I
N
E

Poitiers×

G U I E N N E

Bordeaux   R. Dordogne

G
A
S
C
O
N
Y

R. Rhone

FRANCE
English Miles
0 20 40 60 80 100

Pyrenees

Marseilles

Mediterranean Sea

Emery Walker so

until 1802 all English kings called themselves "Kings of France" and put the French Lilies beside the English Leopards on their Royal Standard. This was the most expensive piece of gardening on record, but the war gave the English a long experience in hard knocks which stood them in good stead.

Edward had in him a good deal of the "knight-errant," the sort of brave, reckless rider who was supposed to go about seeking adventures, rescuing ladies in distress, and cutting the throats of giants. But he had also a rich kingdom at his back and plenty of fighting barons, knights, and freeholders, as greedy of adventure as himself. His subjects, in fact, urged him on and gloried in his splendid series of victories.

The English nation supports him.

Perhaps you are disappointed that I am not going to describe any of his great battles or rides through France; but I had much rather that you learned *why* a King of England was fighting in France than the dates of the Battle of Crecy (1346) or Poitiers (1356). In the open field, up to 1361, we were always victorious. This was because the English leaders, including the King himself, his noble son called the "Black Prince," Chandos, Manny, Knollys, and many others thoroughly understood "tactics" — that is to say, they knew

Battles of Crecy, 1346, Poitiers, 1356.

The Black Prince; his gallant soldiers.

how to move their men on the battlefield.
The French used to huddle too many heavy-
armed knights, whether on horse or foot, into
too small a space, and trusted to crushing the
English by mere weight of numbers. But
it is an old saying that "the thicker the hay is,
the more easy it is to mow it." The French
light infantry was contemptible and was
despised by its own knights; whereas our
sturdy yeomen, armed with the long-bow, were
the first line of every English force and could
pour in such showers of arrows as neither
horses nor men could face. Then our cavalry
could charge in after the arrows had blinded
or frightened whole battalions of the enemy.

Use of the long-bow.

In the course of the war Edward captured
the great city of Calais, which, as you know,
is right opposite Dover. He wanted, or said
that he wanted, to hang six of the principal
citizens of Calais, for the city had made a
desperate resistance and cost him much trouble;
but his good Queen Philippa begged them off.
By the possession of Calais we got command of
the "narrow seas" as we had never had it
before, and Edward III might well put the
picture of a ship on his new gold coins, to show
that he was "Sovereign of the Seas." We held
Calais for 200 years. After more than twenty
years of war Flanders was free from the French,

Capture of Calais, 1347.

Gascony was safe, and, though Scotland was as unconquered as ever, a Scottish king had been taken prisoner at the Battle of Neville's Cross near Durham (1346), and a French king at the Battle of Poitiers. A peace was concluded in 1361, which left Edward in full possession of all the old inheritance of Henry II's wife (Eleanor of Aquitaine), as well as of Calais.

Peace of Bretigny, 1361.

France had been harried from end to end; but so had Northern England by the Scots. And, though our country was gorged with French gold, it was by no means happy. The war had in fact become a war of plunder, which is the worst kind of war. And in 1348 a pestilence, called the Black Death, had swept off more than a third of the population of England, which early in the century had perhaps reached four millions. The exceedingly dirty habits of our ancestors had frequently caused epidemics of various horrible diseases, but never before upon such a scale. No doubt this plague was brought by travellers and goods coming from the East. All Southern Europe suffered, but England perhaps worse than any country. The "villein" class was certainly diminished by one half; and so land-owners could no longer get their labour-rents, or, indeed, get their land tilled at all. Prices

The pestilence of 1348-9.

Results of the pestilence on life and labour.

doubled everywhere, and the few "villeins" that were left demanded enormous wages for a little work. All the "feudal" ties which had bound village life together were snapped. Men began to wander "in search of work" from the old home where they had been born and where their ancestors had lived from earliest Saxon days. Landowners, finding they could get no reapers or threshers, began to sell their land, or take to sheep farming, which wants few hands. Parliament went on saying: "Oh, ye villeins, you *shall* work for the old wages; oh, ye landowners, you *shall not* pay higher ones." But it was not a bit of good. There was a great deal of work to be done; there were very few men to do it, and those men asked and received higher wages. For a year or two it seemed as if society would come to an end.

Last years of Edward III, 1369-77. The Spanish War, 1369-70.

Then, slowly, things got a little better, but, as you shall hear, there was a fierce rebellion of the peasants in the next reign. Edward III's last years were unhappy. His son, the Black Prince, governed Aquitaine, and was beguiled by a Spanish scoundrel, called King Pedro, to interfere in a Spanish civil war. Wherever the Prince and his archers fought they won, but his army suffered dreadfully from the climate. A new King of France took the opportunity to renew the great war (1369)

His captains had been learning tactics from their English foes by the simple process of being beaten till they understood how to hit back, and slowly and patiently began to win back castles and frontier provinces in Aquitaine. The Black Prince, sore stricken with fever, turned every now and then, like a dying leopard, and tore his victorious foes, but in vain. He died in 1376; and his father, King Edward, worn out with hard battles and also with luxurious living between compaigns, died in the next year. The heir was little Richard, son of the Black Prince, aged eleven. Two greedy and unscrupulous uncles, John of Gaunt, Duke of Lancaster, and Thomas, Duke of Gloucester, were glaring at the boy and at each other. So the great reign closed in gloom and fear for the future.

Death of the Black Prince, 1376; and of Edward III, 1377.

CHAPTER VI

THE END OF THE MIDDLE AGES; RICHARD II TO RICHARD III, 1377–1485.

The fifteenth century, a miserable time. As WE go on in English history each period seems to have a character of its own. The twelfth century, in spite of Stephen's reign, is hopeful; the thirteenth is glorious, rich, and fairly peaceful. In the fourteenth begins a decline, of which it is difficult to explain all the causes; both men and classes have begun to snarl at each other. In the fifteenth, the period now before us, they are going to bite each other; the century seems to be a failure all round.

The old society breaking up. The nation at large was by no means rotten; but men's sense of right and wrong had been corrupted by the French and Scottish wars. Too much fighting is as bad for men as too little. Also they were losing their faith in the Church, which had ceased to be the protector of the poor and thought mainly of keeping its enormous riches safe. Men were soon to lose their faith in the Crown as well, and even in the Law. In a rude state of society, when the barons were again becoming too rich and too powerful, and the Crown becoming too poor and too weak, the excellent system of government by Parliament, and even the excellent law courts, were of very little use; the barons used both for their own ends, and they kept armed men to enforce their views.

In those days armies were only raised for particular campaigns, and, when peace came, were disbanded; and the soldiers, who had perhaps been fighting for ten years in France, were not likely to be peaceful when they came home. So they used to attach themselves to some great lord or baron who could employ them in his private quarrels. The numbers of the barons were now very small, but each was proportionately more powerful; and a great man might perhaps hold four or five earldoms. The younger sons of the kings held many of these, and were often the worst rowdies at the fashionable game of "beggar-my-neighbour" and "king of the castle." In my schoolboy days, when we were asked what we knew of any particular baron in the fourteenth or fifteenth century, we usually thought it safe to answer: "He was the King's uncle and was put to death." Most of the King's uncles and cousins

Quarrelsome Earls and Barons.

were put to death, and more of them deserved to be.

As regards the mere "politics" and wars of the hundred and eight years from the accession of Richard II to the death of Richard III, there is little that you need remember.

Richard II, 1377-99; his character. Richard II had many good qualities, but he was rash and hot-headed; while he was a boy his uncles and some four or five other great barons were always trying to rule in his name; when they found this difficult, they conspired against him and killed his best friends. When he came of age they despised him because he kept the peace with France, whereas they and their plundering followers had enjoyed the war. Richard, however, was no coward, and when he was not yet fifteen he had a fine opportunity of showing his pluck. In 1381 the question of the wages of farm labourers, which had been so much upset by the Black Death in 1348, led to a fearful outbreak called the "Peasant Revolt" (1381) all over the richest lands of England. It was headed by one Wat Tyler. London was occupied by the rebels, and King and courtiers had to fly to the Tower. Again the ship of state seemed in danger of foundering; but the peasants lacked real leadership. Young King Richard II (he was then fourteen) showed the greatest pluck

The Peasant Revolt, 1381.

Tyler was killed and the revolt was put down, not without a good deal of hanging. When that was over, men's eyes began to open to the fact that new conditions of life had begun. "Villeinage" was dead; the only labourers left were *free* labourers, who naturally would bargain for the highest wages they could get. Also, much land had ceased to be ploughed and had gone back into pasture for sheep; for wool increased in value every year, and sheep need few hands to guard them.

But for the rest of his reign the King was either chafing against his uncles and their friends, or else planning schemes of vengeance against them. In 1397, after long waiting, he struck swiftly at the leaders of the barons, killing his uncle Thomas and banishing his cousin Henry of Lancaster (son of John of Gaunt, Edward III's third son). Then he got Parliament to pass certain acts which gave him almost absolute power, and all sober men, who reverenced both the Crown and the "Constitution" (which, roughly speaking, means government through Parliament), stood aghast at this.

In 1399 Henry of Lancaster returned, accused Richard of misgovernment, deposed him, and perhaps had him murdered. He then took the crown, and for fourteen years tried to rule

His violence in 1397.

Henry, Duke of Lancaster, becomes King, 1399, as Henry IV, 1399-1413.

England as King Henry IV, but without much
success. The very barons who had aided him
to usurp the throne said he did not reward
them enough; they rose against him and a sort
of civil war began in 1403 and smouldered on
for three or four years. Henry was not a bad
fellow personally; he was devoted to the Church,
and the Church supported him; so did the House
of Commons, which got much power in his
reign. But to keep order, the first task of a

Henry V,
1413-22. King, was too hard a task for him. He died
in 1413. His son Henry V, equally devoted
to the Church, was a much stronger and cleverer
man; there was no civil war in his short reign.
But this was mainly because he put all his
energies into renewing the war with France.

This really was wicked: whatever right

His
attack on
France,
1415. Edward III might have had to the French
crown, Henry V could have none, for he was
not the best living heir of Edward III. The
Earl of March was the best living heir of
Edward III, for he was descended from Edward's *second* son, King Henry V only from
his *third;* but March had been quietly shoved
aside when Henry IV seized the English crown.
However, France was in a worse condition
than England: her King Charles VI was mad,
and her great nobles were tearing each other
and their beautiful country to pieces. Henry

V saw his opportunity and used it without mercy or remorse. He probably thought that such a war would at least draw away all the baronial rowdies and their followers from England, and it did. Henry set about the business of making war in the most practical manner. We owe him one great blessing: he was the first King since the Conquest who began to build a *Royal* fleet, as distinguished from the fleet of the Cinque Ports (which he also kept going); he was the first to use guns on a large scale, both on his ships and with his land army. Guns and gunpowder had been known before the middle of the fourteenth century, but so far had been little used. Their use explains Henry's success in his sieges in France, for with big guns you can batter down stone walls pretty quickly, whereas Edward III had spent eight months over the taking of Calais, which he only won by starving it out.

His fleet and guns.

The French towns defended themselves gallantly, but before his death Henry had managed to conquer all Normandy, and had even reached the River Loire. But his great feat was the glorious Battle of Agincourt, won against enormous odds in 1415. Finally in 1420 he got hold of the poor, mad Charles VI, entered Paris with him and compelled him to conclude the Treaty of Troyes, by which he,

Battle of Agincourt, 1415.

Treaty of Troyes, 1420.

Henry, should succeed to the French crown
and marry the French Princess Katharine.

Death of Henry V, 1422. Then, in the flower of his age, and leaving to
an infant of nine months old the succession
to both crowns, he died in 1422.

Henry VI, 1422-61. The Duke of Bedford continues the French war. There was one good "King's uncle," John,
Duke of Bedford, who did his best to keep these
two crowns on his nephew's head; but there
were other uncles and cousins who were not
so good. Little Henry VI grew up into a
gentle, pious, tender-hearted man, who hated
war, hated wicked courtiers, loved only learning and learned men, founded the greatest
school in the world (Eton), and shut his eyes
to the fact that England was getting utterly
out of hand. Bedford just managed to hold
down Northern France (which had always
hated the Treaty of 1420) until his own death

Joan of Arc. in 1425; after that all Frenchmen rallied to
their natural King, Charles VII. The noble
French "Maid of God," Joan of Arc, came to
lead her people and inspired them with the
belief that God would fight for them if they
would fight bravely for their country. She
was just a peasant-girl of no education, but of
beautiful life and well able to stand hardship;
she believed that the Saints appeared to her
and urged her to deliver France. The French
soldiers came to believe it too, and she led them

ENGLISH ARCHERY WINS AT AGINCOVRT

to battle dressed in full armour and riding astride of a white horse. She allowed no bad language to be used in the army: "If you must swear, Marshal," she said to one of the proudest French nobles, "you may swear by your stick, but by nothing else." The English caught her and burned her as a witch, but she lives in the hearts of all good Frenchmen (and Englishmen) as a saint and a heroine until this day. Step by step the English were driven back till all Normandy, all Aquitaine were lost, and in 1453 nothing remained to us but Calais.

The English driven out of France, 1430-53.

King Henry VI was not sorry; by this time he knew how wicked his father's attack upon France had been. But the fighting instinct of Englishmen was desperately sore; defeat after such victories seemed unbearable. And, while the barons' quarrels round the King's tottering throne became shriller and shriller, there were but too many men in England ready to fight somebody, they did not much care whom so long as there was plunder at the end. Henry's wife, Margaret of Anjou, a fiery, cruel woman, ignored her gentle husband and governed in his name. She had already made herself the partisan of one of the two baronial factions, and had struck down the King's uncle, the Duke of Gloucester. Her favourite minister, the Duke of Suffolk, was actually caught and

Anger of the English; weakness of Henry VI's government.

beheaded by common sailors on board a King's ship as he was flying to France. What should we say if a lot of British sailors now caught and beheaded Mr. Asquith on board the *Dreadnought?* In the same year, 1450, there was a fearful insurrection in Kent, led by a scamp called Jack Cade, who marched into London and beheaded several more of the King's ministers. Law and order were utterly at an end.

Insurrec-
tion of
Jack Cade
1450.

The Duke of York, who was now the best living heir of Edward III, at length took up the cudgels against the House of Lancaster. There was civil war for some six years (1455-61), and battle after battle. The horror of it all had driven the good King, on two occasions, out of his mind. It was *called* the war of the House of York against the House of Lancaster, of the "White Rose" against the "Red Rose"; really, it was the war of some dozen savage barons on one side against another dozen on the other. Each of them had a little army of archers and spearmen; each had perhaps the grudges of a century to pay off upon some rival. The war hardly affected the towns at all, and stopped trade very little, and even the country districts, except in the actual presence of the armies, seem to have suffered little. The growth of wool, at any

The Duke
of York;
the House
of York
and the
House of
Lancaster.

Wars of
the Roses,
1455-61.

rate, and with it the increase of riches, went on as fast as ever. "The King ought to put a *sheep* instead of a *ship* on his coins," was a common saying of the day. Of course the coasts were utterly undefended, and pirates of all sorts had a happy time in the Channel.

If any line of division can be discovered in the country we may say roughly that the North and West were Lancastrian, the South and East (then the richest counties) Yorkist. At last Henry VI was deposed, Queen Margaret took flight and Edward, Duke of York, became King as Edward IV. He was a thoroughly bad man, being cruel, vindictive and, except in warfare, lazy. But Margaret had been vindictive too, and, as regards cruelty, there was little to choose between the parties; after every battle the leaders of the vanquished side were put to death almost as a matter of course.

Edward IV becomes King, 1461.

But, just as Henry IV had quarrelled with the barons who had crowned him, so did Edward IV quarrel with his "Kingmaker" and best friend, the Earl of Warwick. Warwick thereupon deposed Edward and took poor Henry VI, who had been an ill-used prisoner in the Tower of London, and put him back on the throne again. It was only a six months' restoration (1470—1), for Edward returned, slew

The Earl of Warwick, called the Kingmaker

Restoration of Henry VI, 1470-1.

Warwick in battle, slew Henry's only son after the battle, slew all the Lancastrian leaders he could catch, and finally had King Henry murdered in the Tower. After this he "reigned more fiercely than before"; he struck down his own brother George, Duke of Clarence; he employed spies, tortured his prisoners, and hardly called Parliament at all; he took what taxes he pleased from the rich. But he kept order very little better than Henry VI had done. Once he thought he would play the part of a "fine old English King," so he led a great army across to France in 1475, but there allowed himself to be bribed by the cunning Louis XI to go home again without firing a shot. At his death in 1483 his brother, the hunchback Richard, seized the crown, and murdered Edward's two sons (Edward V and Richard, Duke of York) in the Tower. Richard III was a fierce, vigorous villain, and had, in two years and a half, succeeded in murdering a good many nobles, both of the Lancastrian and Yorkist parties.

Finally, all the sober English leaders who still kept their heads began to send secret messages to a famous exiled gentleman, Henry Tudor, Earl of Richmond, who was descended through his mother from the House of Lancaster, begging him to come over from France and upset

Edward IV again, 1471-83.

Edward V 1483; Richard III, 1483-85.

The Earl of Richmond comes to England.

the tyrant. He was to marry Edward IV's daughter Elizabeth, and thus to unite the red and white roses. Henry landed in South Wales with a very small army, which increased as he marched eastward. He met King Richard, defeated and slew him at Bosworth in Leicestershire, 1485. Then he advanced to London and was received with joy and relief as King Henry VII.

Battle of Bosworth 1485.

Apart from the politics and wars of this dreary period there are one or two things to be noticed of much greater interest for us. Every age is only preparation for the next, and the seeds of many of the great "awakenings" of the sixteenth century were sowed in the fifteenth.

The seeds of the Reformation

First, of the religious awakening. We had long been accustomed to growl at the riches of the Church, but, till the end of Edward III's reign, no one had questioned its spiritual powers. No one had doubted that priests could really pardon sin. Men hated the Pope, but no one had yet doubted that he was the "Head of the Church" any more than they had doubted that every priest performed a miracle every time he consecrated the Holy Sacrament. Few had even questioned that by payment of money to Rome you could buy salvation. But the popes, when they got back to Rome in 1415

Hatred of Rome and of the rich churchmen.

after the great "Schism," were little more than Italian bishops, mainly occupied with wars against their neighbours. No doubt their bark was still terrible, but what about their bite? Had they, people wondered, any teeth left to bite with?

John Wyclif.

At the end of Edward III's reign the great English scholar, John Wyclif, began to ask questions about all these things, and to argue that the favourite doctrines of the Roman Church were all comparatively new, that they were not part of Christ's teaching, and could not be found in the Bible at all. He published an English translation of the Bible; hitherto men had only a Latin version of it, and the Church did not encourage laymen to read it. He also founded an order of "poor priests," who were to go about preaching simple Christianity.

The Lollard "heresy."

The English bishops were absolutely terrified, and the monks, abbots, and friars more terrified still. These had long known what greedy eyes laymen cast on their vast wealth. Wyclif, said the great churchmen, was a "heretic," and ought to be burned alive (he died in his

Heretics burned.

bed all safe in 1384). In the reigns of Henry IV and Henry V the clergy persuaded Parliament to make laws saying that heretics *should* be burned alive, and many of Wyclif's followers, during the next hundred and twenty years, were actually so burned. The Church nicknamed them "Lollards," or babblers.

The "State," as represented by the King and Parliament, somewhat unwillingly supported the churchmen in this matter; yet on the whole the State considered that these Lollards were raising dreadful questions, and it would be better to crush them and not allow them the safety-valve of talking. The Church sat on the safety-valve as long as it could; but the steam of free thought was bubbling underneath, and, once it had gathered head enough, would blow those that sat on the safety-valve sky-high into little tiny pieces. When Lollardy bursts forth again in the reign of Henry VIII it will be called by the better name of "Protestantism."

Other changes, too, were not far away. For nearly a thousand years past the nations of Europe had been considered as one great family of which the Pope, and, since 800, some hazy German king who called himself "Roman Emperor," were supposed to be the two heads; other kings were, or ought to be, vassals of these two. The Kings of England and France had never really admitted these large claims, and that was why England and France were ahead of other nations. But all these ideas were

Changes coming all over Europe.

out of date; the spirit of the Crusades was
dead, the *commercial* rivalry of great nations

Gun-
powder. had begun.   Gunpowder was changing the face
of war and was making the strongest and heav-
Printing. iest armour quite useless.   The printing of
books with movable type was discovered about
1459, and, at Westminster, William Caxton
was printing English and Latin books in the
Dis-
covery. reign of Edward IV.   In the same reign certain
Bristol merchants were sailing far into the
Atlantic, to discover half-mythical islands, of
which dim stories, long forgotten, were now
being revived and retold; they did not find
any such islands till the reign of Henry VII
had begun.   Spaniards led by Columbus were
the first to set foot in America in 1492; Portuguese were the first to round the Cape of Good
Hope five years later.   But the idea of new
Greek
earning. worlds to be discovered was in the air.   Finally,
the Turks had taken Constantinople in 1453,
and its exiles, who still spoke a sort of Greek
and possessed many manuscripts of the ancient
Greek philosophers, came to Italy and began
to spread the knowledge of Greek to Western
Europe.

Men
begin to
wake up, Four things, then, were to change the face
of the world — gunpowder, printing, geo-
graphical discovery, and Greek.   They would
lead men first to wonder, then to reflect, and

lastly to question — to question whether all the tales which the Church had been telling the world for a thousand years were true or false. Could Becket's bones really restore a dead man to life? Could a priest turn bread and wine into the actual body and blood of Christ? Was the world really flat and did the sun and moon go round it, as the Church said they did? Might there possibly be other worlds? You can understand, then, that the end of the fifteenth century left men rubbing their eyes, half awake and uneasy, but thinking — thinking hard.

THE DAWN WIND

At two o'clock in the morning if you open your window and listen,
    You will hear the feet of the Wind that is going to call the sun.
And the trees in the shadow rustle and the trees in the moonlight glisten,
    And though it is deep, dark night, you feel that the night is done.

So do the cows in the field. They graze for an hour and lie down,
    Dozing and chewing the cud; or a bird in the ivy wakes,

The hour before the dawn.

Chirrups one note and is still, and the restless
  Wind strays on,
  Fidgeting far down the road, till, softly,
  the darkness breaks.

Back comes the Wind full strength with a
  blow like an angel's wing,
  Gentle but waking the world, as he shouts:
  "The Sun! The Sun!"
And the light floods over the fields and the birds
  begin to sing,
  And the Wind dies down in the grass. It is
  Day and his work is done.

So when the world is asleep, and there seems
  no hope of her waking
  Out of some long, bad dream that makes
  her mutter and moan,
Suddenly, all men arise to the noise of fetters
  breaking,
  And every one smiles at his neighbour and
  tells him his soul is his own!

CHAPTER VII

THE TUDORS AND THE AWAKENING OF ENGLAND, 1485—1603

THE KING'S JOB

Once on a time was a King anxious to under-
stand
What was the wisest thing a man could do for
his land.
Most of his population hurried to answer the
question,
Each with a long oration, each with a new sug-
gestion.
They interrupted his meals, he wasn't safe in
his bed from 'em.
They hung round his neck and heels, and at last
His Majesty fled from 'em.
He put on a leper's cloak (people leave lepers
alone),
Out of the window he broke, and abdicated his
throne.
All that rapturous day, while his Court and his
Ministers mourned him,

He danced on his own highway till his own
policemen warned him.

Gay and cheerful he ran (lepers don't cheer
as a rule)

Till he found a philosopher-man teaching an
infant school.

The windows were open wide, the King sat
down on the grass,

And heard the children inside reciting "Our
King is an ass."

The King popped in his head, "Some people
would call this treason,

But I think you are right," he said; "will you
kindly give me your reason?"

Lepers in school are rare as kings with a leper's
dress on,

But the class didn't stop or stare; it calmly
went on with the lesson:

*"The wisest thing, we suppose, that a man can
do for his land,*

*Is the work that lies under his nose, with the
tools that lie under his hand."*

The King whipped off his cloak and stood in
his crown before 'em.

He said: "My dear little folk, *Ex ore parvulorum*
(Which is Latin for 'Children know more than
grown-ups would credit').

You have shown me the road to go, and I
propose to tread it."

Back to his Kingdom he ran, and issued a
    Proclamation,
"Let every living man return to his occupa-
    tion!"
Then he explained to the mob that cheered in
    his palace and round it,
"I've been to look for a job, and Heaven be
    praised I've found it!"

Now we come to a very different part of
history, the period when our own modern
world began to be born. It was a dreadful
stretch of years because the breaking up of
the old ideas of religion, of geography and of
trade was accompanied by great suffering to
many classes and by the loss of many noble
lives of those who clung to the old ideas. Yet
it was a splendid period because of the close
union and understanding between the new
Tudor kings and their people; because England armed herself to face dangers from foreign
foes so resolutely that, at the end of it, she was
the first sea-power in the world. And it was
a time in which England produced a series of
really great men in every walk of life. Men's
minds were stirred up to think, and so the men
with the greatest minds came to the front;

The Sixteenth century; an awakened world.

Struggle between old and new ideas.

The old order changeth, giving place to new,
And God fulfils Himself in many ways.

Wyclif had done little more than prepare
the bed in which the seed was to be sowed,
the seed of knowledge and of the "Spirit which
giveth life." England was, as she is still, a
deeply conservative country; our people were
slow at taking up new ideas, and too much in
love with money. They wanted kings who
would give them peace and order, knock down
the great nobles, restrict or even abolish the
Pope's power. But they did not at first want
"heresy" or wish to break with the Catholic
Church of their fathers.

Henry
VII, 1485-
1509; his
task;

Henry VII was a King admirably suited to
carry out some of these wishes. If you gave
him a name you would call him "Henry the
Prudent." He did not do as did the king in
the poem on page 129, nor did any *real* king
of whom I ever heard; but Henry tried hard
to find out what a king's real "job" should be,
and he set to work to do it; moreover, he did
his best to make Englishmen stop talking and
fighting among themselves, and set them to
work each at his own job. His claim to the
throne was not a very good one, and his aim
therefore was to "let sleeping dogs lie." "Mind
your own businesses, my dear subjects, and
let me mind mine," was what he said to himself. His main task was to heal the wounds
left by the civil war; and, in a reign of twenty-

four years, he had almost completely healed
them. There were at first some small insur-
rections, after-swells of the late storm, but
they were put down with ease. Henry called
few parliaments and asked for little money,
but heaped up treasure by other ways. He
taxed rich people, though he had no legal his caution;
right to do so; he carefully nursed trade and
manufacture; and he imposed enormous fines
on all big men who broke his laws, especially
his laws which forbade them to keep large
bands of retainers who would fight their quarrels.
His ministers and privy councillors were either
bishops or middle-class laymen; and the Privy
Council became almost more important than
Parliament. He cut off few heads, but chose
them wisely, for those he did cut off were
the most dangerous. A great monarchy was
growing up in Spain as well as in France; even his love of peace.
Germany was trying hard to be a united coun-
try. Henry watched them all, and made
numerous treaties with them, but refused to
be led into expense or adventures; above all
he avoided wars. With Scotland he kept firm
peace, the first real peace since 1290, and he
married his daughter Margaret to King James
IV; it was the great-grandson of this marriage,
who, as James I, finally united the two countries in 1603. As for the Church, it also seemed

to be wrapped in profound peace; the mutterings against it were all under the surface.

Yet before Henry died the "New Learning," which was to lead to the Reformation, was in full swing in England. Great scholars like John Colet and Thomas More were reading the Scriptures in their original Greek, and finding out how very much the Roman Church differed from the earliest forms of Christianity. The study of Greek had begun at both universities, and English scholars were continually travelling to Germany and Italy.

In 1509 Henry died, and was succeeded by his son Henry VIII, aged eighteen, a most splendid young man, of great natural cleverness and devoted to the New Learning, but devoted also to every sort of game, pleasure and extravagance. For the business of the State he at first cared nothing. "Oh, go and talk to my

Chancellor about that," he would say. His Chancellor was the cunning Thomas Wolsey, afterward Cardinal, Archbishop of York and Legate (*i. e.* special agent) of the Pope. Wolsey got all power into his own hands and managed things badly. He allowed his master to waste the treasures heaped up by Henry VII, and, when the King called Parliaments, they growled at this extravagance, and refused to vote the huge sums for which he asked them.

He plunged into foreign politics, and made a foolish war with France, which at once broke the long peace with Scotland; for James IV invaded England with a huge army, which was defeated by Henry's general, the Earl of Surrey, at Flodden Field (1513). Wolsey realized that the Church was in danger, both from the New Learning and from the growing outcry against its riches, and he was most anxious to put off any open attack on it; but as for reform he had no plans.

War with Scotland, battle of Flodden, 1513.

The storm broke first in Germany, where, in 1517, the simple monk, Martin Luther, began by attacking some of the more scandalous abuses of the Church, and ended, a year or two later, by declaring the Pope to be "Antichrist." Henry VIII professed himself to be deeply shocked at this, wrote a book in defence of the Catholic doctrines, and forbade Englishmen to read Luther's books. But these books, and many others upon the same side, could not be kept out of England, and nothing could prevent eager young men from reading them. By the year 1527 there was a small but vigorous body of scholars in England who were prepared to attack the teaching of the old Church as well as its riches. They called themselves "Protestants"; their enemies called them "heretics." Their main cry was for the

The Reformation in Germany, 1517; it begins to influence England, 1520-30.

The First "Protestants."

Bible as the ground of all Christian teaching;
"away with everything that cannot be found
in the Bible."

Henry
seeks a
divorce,
1527.
Until 1527 the Government sternly repressed
every movement against the Pope. Then a
purely political event caused it to turn round.
King Henry wanted to divorce his wife Katharine, a Spanish princess, who had been the wife
of his brother Arthur. Arthur had died in 1501.
The Pope had allowed Henry to marry Katharine, although many people had doubted
whether such a marriage could possibly be
lawful. Only one child of this marriage,
Princess Mary, born 1516, had survived, and
Henry thought, or professed to think, that
this was a "judgment of God" on him. Also
he wanted to marry some one else, the Lady
Anne
Boleyn.
Anne Boleyn, one of Queen Katharine's court
ladies. He applied to the Pope for a divorce.
Popes were in the bad habit of doing these
little jobs to please kings; but Pope Clement
VII would not do this. King Charles of Spain
and Germany, called the "Emperor," was the
nephew of Queen Katharine; he was much the
most powerful monarch in Europe, and Clement
Henry
and Pope
Clement
VII, 1527-
29.
dared not offend him. So the Pope, and Wolsey for him, shifted and twisted and turned
and promised, but could not give the King
of England his wishes.

Suddenly, to the surprise of all his courtiers, of all England, of all Europe, Henry roared out, "Pope! What do I care for the Pope? Call my Parliament!"

It was the year 1529. The King was thirty-eight years old, and quite unknown to his people, except from the rumours of his extravagance. Suddenly he appeared before them as their leader and friend, prepared to do all, and more than all, on which their hearts were set. The nation had hardly dared to whisper its desire to curb the Pope and the Church; here was a King who shouted it aloud!

The Parliament of 1529-36.

Union of King and People.

Do not think that I praise Henry VIII. It was a selfish and wicked motive that started the idea in his mind. What I say is that, once the idea was started, he would have all the Kings of Europe against him, and no friend but his own people; and so King and people now became one as they had never been before.

Very few Englishmen were as yet prepared to accept any new sort of Church; most of them hated the idea of "heresy." Henry hated it also, and continued to the end of his life to burn a few extreme heretics. King and people wished no more than to abolish the power of the Pope in England, to strip the Church of its enormous wealth, and yet

What the Nation desired.

to remain "good Catholics." Was this possible? History was to prove that it was not; once the Pope was pulled down in England a "Reformation" of *all* the Church in England must follow, in spite of any effort to prevent it. Henry just managed to stave off this reformation while he lived.

The Laws against the Pope, 1529-36.

The Parliament of 1529 sat for seven years and when it rose a new England had begun. How the new laws against the Church were forced through the House of Lords no one knows; one fears it was by terror and threats, for nearly all the bishops and certainly all the abbots would be against them; and of the forty-five lay peers, a strong minority must have hated serious changes. But the House of Commons, almost to a man, welcomed these changes; and that House then represented the sober country gentlemen and the sober merchants of England.

One by one all the powers of the Pope were shorn away, the power of making laws for themselves was taken from the clergy, the Church was declared to be independent of any foreign influence, but wholly dependent on the Crown. Every one was obliged to swear that the King was the "Head of the Church." The new

Archbishop Cranmer.

Archbishop of Canterbury, Thomas Cranmer, pronounced the divorce from Katharine, and

married his King to Anne Boleyn; the Princess
Mary was set aside, and when Anne's daughter,
the Princess Elizabeth, was born, she was
declared heir to the throne. All the smaller
monasteries were dissolved and their lands
handed over to the Crown; Henry gave most
of them to his courtiers and to important
country gentlemen, and so a new set of nobles,
newly enriched from Church lands and entirely
dependent on the King, rapidly came to the
front. *Monasteries dissolved.*

Many of the best men in Fngland were
deeply shocked at these changes, even some
who had been prepared to go a long way in re-
forming the abuses of the Church. But Henry
and his savage minister, Thomas Cromwell,
struck down every one who stood in their
path. The Courtenays and Poles, descended
from Edward IV, were imprisoned, or driven
into exile, or had their heads cut off. Sir
Thomas More, once the King's intimate friend,
and Bishop Fisher of Rochester, both men of
European fame for their learning and piety,
were the most distinguished victims. In the
North of England, in 1536, a fierce insurrection
broke out called the "Pilgrimage of Grace";
the rebels cried out for the restoration of the
monasteries, for in that wild country the monks
had been the only doctors and their houses
Thomas Cromwell; fierce measures against the old Church and the old nobles.
Pilgrimage of Grace, 1536.

had been open to all travellers. The rising
was put down with great cruelty, for Henry
was naturally a cruel man, and he was now
drunk with pride and power.

Birth of
Prince
Edward,
1537.

He had already beheaded his second wife,
Anne, and married his third, Jane Seymour;
she bore to him in 1537 a son, afterward
Edward VI, and died a few days afterward.
In the last seven years of his life he married
three more wives, one of whom he divorced,
another he beheaded, and the third survived
him.

The new
land-
owners.

In 1539 the remaining monasteries, even
the greatest, were dissolved and, as a result,
the great abbots ceased to attend Parliament.
Some of their wealth was used to found schools
and professorships at Oxford and Cambridge
and to create six new bishoprics; but most of
it went to the nobles and gentlemen. Thus,
within three years, nearly a quarter of the land
of England had got new owners. All the great
offices of state had been wholly taken away
from churchmen, and were now in the hands

The Con-
fessions
of Faith.

of these new nobles. New "Confessions of
Faith" (declaring what was the true teaching
of the Church of England) were published;
first the "Ten Articles," then the "Six Articles";
the former was a step in the direction of the
German Protestantism; the latter was very

HOW HENRY VIII HAD THE MONKS TURNED OUT OF THE MONASTERIES

nearly the old Catholic faith but without the
Pope; and I must repeat that it was this mid-
way position which, as late as Henry's own
death, most people in England preferred.

But Henry had ordered an English trans- The English Bible.
lation of the Bible to be placed in every parish
church for every one to read, and in 1544
he allowed the Litany to be said in English;
this was really the beginning of our beloved
Prayer Book.   And, once lay Englishmen began
to read the Bible for themselves, they would
not long be content to believe in confession
to a priest or in the miracle of the Mass (both
of which were taught in the Six Articles).

Now all these changes were carried through Danger of foreign invasion on behalf of the Pope.
under continued danger from abroad, for of
course the Pope had declared Henry to be deposed, and called on all Catholic princes to go
and depose him.   Much of the danger was
from the old alliance of France and Scotland,
but far more from the power of Spain, Germany,
and Flanders, now all in the hands of the
Emperor, Charles V.   Threats of invasion were
incessant, but Henry armed his people to the Henry arms his people.
teeth, and, at the end of his reign, had a navy
of seventy ships ready for action.   He built
castles all round his southern and eastern coasts,
and was always making great guns to put in
them.   He knew that the few remaining de-

scendants of Edward III were plotting to upset
his throne, especially the exiled Reginald Pole,
a great favourite of the Pope. He had already
sliced off the heads of all his royal cousins
whom he could catch. With the approval of
his Parliament, he had settled that the crown
should go after his death to his son Edward;
if Edward had no children, to Mary; then,
if Mary had no children, to Elizabeth; lastly,
if all three of his children died without direct
heirs, it was to go to the heirs of his younger
sister, Mary, Duchess of Suffolk, not to those
of his elder sister, Margaret, Queen of Scotland. He hated Scotland as bitterly as Edward
I, and continued the Border wars as fiercely
until his death in 1547.

Thus you will say I have drawn for you the
picture of a monster of cruelty and selfishness?
Yes, Henry was just that. But he was also
something much more. He was a great patriot,
a great Englishman. He taught Englishmen
to rely on themselves and their ships; and
he taught future English kings to rely on their
people. He shivered in pieces the foreign yoke
that had bound the Church of England since
Saint Augustine had preached in the open air
to the early Kings of Kent. Great suffering
accompanied these great changes; and they
were thoroughly bad for the moral character

Who should succeed Henry?

Henry's charac-ter.

Sufferings of the poor.

THE HENRY GRACE A DIEU called THE GREAT HARRY HENRY'S BIGGEST SHIP

HENRY VIII · SEES THAT ENGLAND HAS A GOOD FLEET.

of the generation which saw them. The new landowners were men who thought only of riches, and turned out the tenants of the old monks by the score, and by the hundred. A swarm of beggars were let loose over the country, beggars to whom the monks had given daily doles of bread and beer. Savage laws of whipping and forced labour had to be passed to keep these men in order. Moreover, since the discovery by the Spaniards of rich gold and silver mines in America, money had come into Europe in great floods and this had sent up the price of all goods at a fearful rate; all trade seemed uncertain; great fortunes might be suddenly made, and as suddenly lost. So the strong and the clever (and often the wicked) prospered, and the weak and the old-fashioned people were ruined.

Greed of the rich.

The six years' reign of the boy Edward VI (1547—53) only made all this social misery worse. Every one had been afraid of Henry VIII; no one was afraid of a child of ten, though he was a clever and strong-willed child. The result was that the government became a scramble for wealth and power among the new nobles, the Seymours, Dudleys, Russells, Herberts, Greys, and many more who had been enriched with abbey lands. It was the fear of losing these lands and the desire of confiscating for

Edward VI, 1547-53.

Scramble of the new nobles for riches and power.

themselves what remained of Church property that drove these men, quite against the wishes of sober people, to force on a reformation of the teaching of the Church. The result in the long run was good, because the Protestant faith did then first get a lawful footing in England; but the result for the moment was bad, because moderate men began to mistrust a Reformation which seemed to be bound up with greed for spoil and with contempt for all the past traditions of England. At the same time the leaders of the new Protestant Church were all men of high character. Cranmer, Ridley, Latimer, and Hooper, all bishops of King Edward, all died for their faith in the next reign.

They degrade the Reformation.

However much we may rightly abuse the greedy nobles, we can never wholly regret a reign which first gave us the Prayer Book in English and substituted the Communion for the Mass. Cranmer prepared two successive Prayer Books, the second (1552) somewhat more Protestant than the first of 1549, and it was the second which, with very slight alterations, became our present Prayer Book in the reign of Elizabeth. In Edward's reign also the marriage of priests was allowed, and the laws about burning heretics were abolished. In his reign too, alas, the beautiful stained-

The two Prayer Books of Edward VI, 1549 and 1552.

glass windows, statues and pictures were removed from most of our churches, whose walls were now covered with whitewash.

Edward's first Regent or "Protector" was his mother's brother, Edward Seymour, Duke of Somerset; a man of much higher character than most of the nobles, but rash and hotheaded, and quite unfit to lead the nation. He continued Henry's vindictive quarrel with Scotland, won a great victory at Pinkie, and drove the Scots once more into the arms of France. Their girl-queen, Mary Stuart, who might have been a bride for our boy-king, was sent for safety to France and married to the French King's son. Somerset was soon upset by a much more violent person, the ruffian John Dudley, Duke of Northumberland, who pushed on the Reformation at greater speed for purely selfish ends, and disgusted all sober men with it. He brought in a lot of foreign Protestants and gave them places in the English Church; he brought in foreign troops to be his bodyguard, bullied the Princess Mary (who was the natural head of the Catholic party), thrust all the leading Catholics into prison, and tossed the remaining Church lands to his fellow nobles.

But Edward, who had always been very delicate, began early in 1553 to draw near his

The Duke of Somerset, Protector.

His quarrel with Scotland, 1548.

The Duke of Northumberland, 1550-53.

Violence of the Reformers.

Edward VI, very ill.

end. Mary's succession was sure, and, though no one knew exactly what line she would take in religious matters, it was certain that she would stop the violent progress of the Reformation, and quite certain that she would kill Northumberland. So the Duke persuaded the dying boy-king, now sixteen, to make a will, passing over both his sisters, and leaving the crown to his cousin, Lady Jane Grey, heiress of the Suffolk line and recently married to one of Northumberland's sons. When Edward died in July, Jane was actually proclaimed Queen in London.

His death 1553.

Jane Grey.

But not a cheer was raised by the crowd, and the whole nation rose as one man for the injured Princess Mary. Within nine days Jane was a prisoner in the Tower, where a few months afterward she was executed, and Mary rode into London with her sister Elizabeth at her side.

Mary I, 1553-8; her character.

Mary's reign of five years and four months is the greatest tragedy in our history. She was a good woman, passionately attached to the Catholic faith and to the memory of her mother. She was learned, clever and of lofty courage. But she was a Spaniard at heart and never an Englishwoman. Like a Spaniard she was vindictive, and, unfortunately, she had deep wrongs to avenge.

Yet, if Protestantism were to triumph in the long run, something of the fearful cruelty she was going to inflict upon it was necessary; for moderate men had hitherto mainly seen it as the religion of a gang of selfish nobles seeking to divide all the riches of England among themselves. Nine tenths of England preferred anything — almost the Pope — to Northumberland and his land-grabbing crew. At the least, they wanted a return to the state of things at the end of Henry's reign. "No foreigners," was the cry; "England and English Church for the English." *The Reformation in danger.*

But Mary cared little for her countrymen, cared only for her Church; she was determined to restore the state of things which had existed at the beginning, not at the end, of her father's reign; to restore the Pope and all his works, and to do this by making the closest alliance with the Emperor Charles and his son Philip, whom she determined, against all good advice, to marry. In six months she had terrified her people; in two years she had completely lost their hearts; in six years she had wrecked forever the Catholic faith in the minds of intelligent Englishmen. *Mary no Englishwoman; her marriage to Philip of Spain.*

She hurled all the leaders of the Reformed Church into prison at once, and set about reestablishing the Catholic services everywhere. *Catholic faith set up again.*

The greedy nobles, one and all, now professed themselves to be good Catholics, and them she dared not touch. The one thing they feared was to lose their new grants of the abbey lands. They knew the Queen was bent upon restoring the monasteries, and the laws for burning heretics, which had been abolished in the reign of Edward VI; but she was not able to persuade her Parliaments to do the latter until the end of 1554, and the lands she was never able to touch at all. But Reginald Pole, long an exile and now a Cardinal, came over as "Legate" of the Pope, and in the Pope's name absolved England from the guilt of heresy. Mary had already been married to Prince Philip of Spain.

The Protestant martyrs, 1555-8.

The burnings of the Protestant martyrs began early in 1555, and in less than three years nearly three hundred persons were burned at the stake. The burnings were nearly all in the south-eastern counties, which shows us that Protestantism had got the strongest hold on what were then the richest and most intelligent parts of England; the north and west long remained Catholic. The four great Protestant bishops, Cranmer, Ridley, Latimer and Hooper, were among the victims; but three fourths of these victims were persons in quite humble life. The people of those days were well used to look on at all sorts of cruel tortures at executions, and were quite unfeeling on the subject; but the high courage with which these martyrs met their terrible deaths made an impression that has never been forgotten. So it was the reign of "Bloody Mary," not that of Edward VI, that was the true birthday of Protestanism in England.

And no great Englishman approved of the burnings; it was only the Spanish councillors and the Queen herself who urged them on. It was felt to be "a foreigners' job," and the hatred for Spain and all its works soon came to outweigh the old hatred for France.

A "Spanish job"; hatred of Englishmen for Spain.

This hatred became much more fierce when Philip dragged England into one of his frequent wars with France, and when the cunning Frenchmen seized the opportunity to make a spring upon Calais (which we had held since Edward III), and captured it. The loss of Calais seemed an indelible shame. All the last two years of Mary's reign revolts were on the point of breaking out. French ships full of English Protestant exiles prowled in the Channel and harried Spanish and English trade. No heir was born to the throne, though Mary, who was slowly dying of dropsy, kept hoping for a baby. Philip showed her no love

Loss of Calais, 1558.

Death of Mary, 1558.

and little civility. Her reign had been a nightmare of terror, and it closed amid loss, ruin, pestilence, and famine.

Elizabeth, 1558-1603. The Princess Elizabeth, who then came to the throne in November 1558, was a very different person to her sister. Her life had been several times in great danger during Mary's reign, and the Spanish councillors had *Her charac-ter.* often urged Mary to put her to death. She was a woman of the most strangely varied character; extraordinarily stingy and mean, extraordinarily brave and fierce (not cruel); passionately fond of her country, and English to the backbone; so jealous that she could not bear her courtiers to look at another woman; so vain of her beauty that even in old age she covered herself with gorgeous dresses and ridiculous jewels; by turns a scold, a flirt, a cheat and a heroine. But, somehow or other, she made her people follow, obey, and worship her, till at last she became a sort of crowned spirit and guardian angel of the whole nation, which felt that it had grown to full manhood and *"Glori-ana."* power under her protecting care. Men called her "Gloriana."

Her position and that of her people was, at *Her danger and that of England.* her accession, one of great danger. England was entirely without allies, and, owing to the bad management of the two last reigns, almost bankrupt. Catholic Europe and many Catholics in England considered that the Queen had no right to the throne, for they had never approved of her father's marriage to Anne Boleyn. The true Queen of England, they thought, was Mary Queen of Scots. So thought that young and beautiful lady herself, and, in Elizabeth's first year, Mary became Queen of France as well. Indeed, the prospect of the union of France, Scotland, and England in one hand thoroughly frightened King Philip of Spain, and made him for many years more friend than foe to Elizabeth.

Mary Stuart, Queen of Scots.

He, therefore, in 1558, implored Elizabeth to keep England Catholic and to marry some decent Catholic Prince. But her sister's reign had killed Catholicism in the hearts of all the best and most vigorous of the younger men in England; she knew this, and so, though she dreaded the extreme Protestants and loved the gorgeous services of the old Church, she rightly decided that she must reign as a Protestant Queen. Yet the difficulties of settling the new Church were enormous; she had to make bishops of men who had fled abroad to escape death; and many of the most eager Protestants now objected to bishops altogether, while many more disliked even the very moderate services of the Prayer Book of 1552. Such men were

The religious settlement of England.

A Protestant Queen.

the germ of the party soon to be called "Puritans," and, in later days, "Dissenters" or "Nonconformists." *Moderation*, then, was the Queen's watchword; to build up a Church which should offend as few and please as many as possible. Her great adviser for forty years was the wise William Cecil, afterward Lord Burghley, the most far-seeing and moderate of men. And the Queen and Cecil and their Parliament had, in five years — say by 1563 — built the Church upon such broad foundations that it has remained, with few changes, our own "Church of England" until this day. Laws were passed in Parliament making Elizabeth "Supreme Governor" of this Church, making the Prayer Book (very slightly altered from the edition of 1552) the only lawful service book, and publishing the present "Thirty-nine Articles" as the Confession of Faith. Year by year more and more people rallied to this Church, and Parliament was able to pass stronger and stronger laws against those who refused to conform to it, whether Catholics or Puritans.

All her reign, but especially for the first twenty-eight years of it, the Queen was in constant danger of being murdered by some extreme Catholic agent of the Pope. Such men called her "heretic," "bastard," "usurper,"

Margin notes:
William Cecil, Lord Burghley.

The Prayer Book.

The Thirty-nine Articles.

Plots against the Queen's life.

and other ugly names. There was plot after plot, and the Catholics, perhaps not unnaturally, considered the traitors who were executed for these plots to be martyrs, not murderers. But, as each plot failed, the main result was to drive all moderate Catholics into the English Church; for most of them, much as they had deplored the "heresy" of their Queen, were patriots at heart.

Elizabeth hated war, partly because she had a shrewd idea that England was hardly strong or rich enough to engage in a great foreign war, but still more because she simply couldn't bear to pay her soldiers and sailors. In fact, she expected her subjects to fight her battles for her by taking service with rebellious Scottish, French or Spanish subjects, while she pretended to be at peace with the sovereigns of those countries. But she was often obliged to send small and almost secret expeditions to help these rebels. Philip of Spain, for instance, was engaged in a long and desperate attempt to suppress Protestantism in the "Low Countries" (the modern Belgium and Holland), and our Queen was constantly sending aid to the Protestants there, though never openly till 1585, by which time the "Dutch Republic" had been born there, and had become the most valuable ally of England.

Stinginess of the Queen.

She helps foreigners to rebel, but secretly.

The Dutch.

It was the same story in France, where a strong Protestant party, continually fed by underhand help from England, kept up a civil war for thirty years. All this weakened the two great Catholic powers, and made Elizabeth stand out more and more as the Champion of European Protestantism.

On the whole, however, her reign is mainly occupied with two long duels, that with Mary, Queen of Scots, 1560–87, and that with Philip of Spain, which began to be severe about 1570 and lasted till her death.

The long rivalry with Mary Stuart.

The beautiful Mary Stuart returned, a widowed Queen, to Scotland in 1561 to find that Elizabeth had already helped the Scottish nobles to overthrow the French power and the Catholic Church at one blow. The new Church that was then set up in Scotland was called the "Presbyterian" from its government by "presbyters" or elders instead of bishops, and was far more violently Protestant than ours. This is important to remember because, to those English Puritans who wanted to abolish bishops and the Prayer Book in our own Church, the example of Scotland was always present. Mary was a clever woman, but quite without principles, and far more reckless than her English rival. She honestly believed herself to be rightful Queen of England, but she found it hard work to keep

The Reformation in Scotland.

The English Puritans.

her own crown, and in six years she had lost
it. For she was always an object of suspicion
to the Scottish nobles, both as a Catholic and
as a Frenchwoman at heart. She married her
cousin, Lord Darnley, in 1565, and bore him
a son, who afterward, as James I, united the
two crowns of Britain. Then, in 1567, Mary
allowed her husband to be murdered and
married his murderer, the Earl of Bothwell.
Scotland rose in wrath, deposed and imprisoned
her, crowned her baby son, and had him
brought up as a Protestant King. A year
later Mary escaped from prison and fled to
England, demanding aid from her rival
Elizabeth.

Flight of Mary to England, 1568.

That clever lady pretended to pity Mary,
but kept her safe, at first as a sort of guest,
soon as a prisoner for nineteen dreary years.
No wonder that Mary soon began to plot
against Elizabeth's life, and to implore the
aid of every Catholic power in Europe. The
one insurrection of Elizabeth's reign, that of
the North of England in 1569, was got up in
order to put Mary on the throne. At last,
in despair, Elizabeth's wisest councillors implored her to bring Mary to trial; and in 1587,
the Scottish Queen was tried, condemned and
beheaded in Fotheringay Castle.

Mary in custody in England; her plots.

Her trial and death, 1587.

This was an open challenge on the part of

Spain will avenge her.

England to Catholic Europe. Mary had made a will in which she passed over her son, left Philip of Spain heir to both her crowns and implored him to avenge her. He was ready to do so, for he had long been tired of Elizabeth's secret aid to his rebels, and exasperated at the failure of the plotters to kill the English Queen. So he prepared to send against us a great fleet, known to history as the "Spanish Armada."

The English Navy,
Now Henry VII and Henry VIII had been the real makers of the English navy, for they had been the first kings to build big ships which could sail anywhere and fight anybody. And Henry VIII had paid very special attention to guns and gunnery. He had also been the true father of English merchant shipping, and had encouraged his subjects to trade to distant and English merchant-ships.
parts of the world. All merchant-ships in those days carried guns, for they always had to be ready for a tussle with pirates. So, though the Spanish fleet was perhaps twice as numerous as the English *Royal* navy, the number of fighting ships that England could put to sea far out-numbered those that Spain could send into the Channel. And our men were going to fight, not only for Queen and faith, but for home and wives and children; to fight, too, on their own shores, every tide and shoal of which was well known to them.

When Spain had discovered America and Spanish America; the Portuguese had found the way round the Portuguese India. Cape of Good Hope to India, each tried to exclude all other nations from the seas they had explored, from the lands they had discovered, and from the trades they had opened up. And a Pope had had the astounding insolence to divide these seas, countries, and trades between the Spaniards and Portuguese, giving the Western World to Spain, the Eastern to Portugal. Englishmen, when they abolished English sailors in America. the Pope, naturally laughed at this exclusion; they meant to take, and did take, English goods to all countries where they could find a market for them, and this rough, deep-sea game went on all through the reigns of Edward and Mary. In the reign of Elizabeth it became *the* game of Englishmen. You can imagine some simple English sailor lad, who had perhaps never done more than a few coasting voyages from one little port of Devon to another, opening his eyes to the wonders of the Tropics as he sails in Francis Drake's great voyage in the *Golden* Drake's voyage round the world, 1577-80. *Hind* across the Atlantic, across the Equator, south and ever south till the Strait of Magellan opens the door into the Pacific; then north again, picking up here and there some rich Spanish merchant-ship as a prize; then across through innumerable spice islands to the Indian

Ocean, and so round the Cape of Good Hope
and home; home to his own wind-swept Channel
and the white cliffs by Plymouth. This was
in 1580 — the first English voyage round the
World, the third only of such voyages in re-
corded history; honour to Sir Francis Drake!

WITH DRAKE IN THE TROPICS

South and far south below the Line,
   Our Admiral leads us on,
Above, undreamed-of planets shine —
   The stars we knew are gone.
Around, our clustered seamen mark
   The silent deep ablaze
With fires, through which the far-down shark
   Shoots glimmering on his ways.

The sultry tropic breezes fail
   That plagued us all day through;
Like molten silver hangs our sail,
   Our decks are dark with dew.
Now the rank moon commands the sky,
   Ho! Bid the watch beware
And rouse all sleeping men that lie
   Unsheltered in her glare.

How long the time 'twixt bell and bell!
   How still our lanthorns burn!

How strange our whispered words that tell
  Of England and return!
Old towns, old streets, old friends, old loves,
  We name them each to each.
While the lit face of Heaven removes
  Them farther from our reach.

Now is the utmost ebb of night
  When mind and body sink,
And loneliness and gathering fright
  O'erwhelm us, if we think —
Yet, look, where in his room apart,
  All windows opened wide,
Our Admiral thrusts away the chart
  And comes to walk outside.

Kindly, from man to man he goes,
  With comfort, praise, or jest.
Quick to suspect our childish woes,
  Our terror and unrest.
It is as though the sun should shine —
  Our midnight fears are gone!
South and far south below the Line,
  Our Admiral leads us on!

Drake, Hawkins, Raleigh, Grenville, Cavendish and a hundred more of gallant English merchants and sailors pushed their ships and their trade into every corner of Spanish America;

and of course the Spaniards hanged many of them as pirates and burned others as heretics. Remonstrances to the English Queen were of little use, for she was often able to reply to Philip, "Then why is your Majesty encouraging plots against my life and helping my rebels in Ireland?"

The Spanish Armada, 1588.

Philip had, in fact, delayed his attack too long; he had no idea how strong England had grown in the thirty years of Elizabeth's reign. And though he was now King of Portugal as well as Spain, and master of all the gold mines of America, he was as stingy as Elizabeth. Even in this critical year, 1588, his "Armada" was not nearly big enough to win, and it was very badly equipped as a fighting force; his ships did not carry enough gunpowder, and most of their provisions were rotten. Still, the terror was great in many English hearts as the Spaniards swept up channel in the last half of July. For one long, hot week our light and swift sailing ships hung round their flanks, knocking their spars to pieces at long range, almost without the loss of a single English life or gun. The object of the Spaniards was to avoid fighting until they came off the Dutch coast, for there was a large Spanish army collected in the River Scheldt, under the great General Parma, ready to be ferried across to

AT THE TIME OF THE ARMADA ~ ~ ~
ELIZABETH REVIEWS THE TROOPS AT TILBURY

the mouth of the Thames. But before the Spaniards reached the Straits of Dover their fleet had been half crippled by the English guns; and, when they were off Calais, a lot of boats smeared with pitch and full of gunpowder were set on fire and set adrift among them. This so terrified the Spanish Admiral that he put his whole fleet about and fled into the North Sea. Then great gales arose and drove them northward and ever northward. Many were wrecked, the remainder lumbered round Scotland and southward again round Ireland; perhaps half or one third, and these, mostly mere hulks, arrived at length in the harbours of Spain; the winds and waves and rocks had finished what the English guns had begun:

Long, long in vain the waiting mothers kneel
In the white palaces of far Castile.
Weep, wide brown eyes that watch along the
    shore,
Your dark-haired lovers shall return no
    more;
Only it may be, on the rising tide,
The shattered hull of one proud bark may
    glide,
To moor at even on a smooth bay's breast,
Where the South mountains lean toward the
    West,

> A wraith of battle with her broken spars,
> Between the water's shimmer and the stars.*

England and Protestantism saved. Our country, and, with her, the great cause of freedom and Protestantism, were saved. Spain was now known to be mainly a bugbear to frighten children, and England and Elizabeth ruled the waves.

The last years of Elizabeth, 1589-1603. The great Queen lived for fifteen years after her victory, and her enemy, Philip, lived for ten. She never realized how complete that victory had been; when her best councillors and her bravest sailors urged her to follow it up and blow the Spanish once and for all out of the seas, she utterly refused. She allowed occasional raids on the Spanish coasts and colonies, and one of these took the city and burned the great dockyard of Cadiz; but pay for a big war she would not; though, in a big war, swift victory was all but certain, and would have produced a lasting peace. Her last years were very lonely; she had never married; the great men who had helped her to make England a first-rate power, Burghley, Walsingham, Drake, **Her successor.** Grenville, had died before her. The rising generation was all looking toward her successor, and that could only be King James of Scotland, whom she cordially hated, and whom she knew

---

* Sir James Rennell Rodd: Oxford Prize Poem, 1880, "Raleigh."

to be incapable of continuing her work. The Church of England, which she had nursed, was indeed safe; but the Puritan party within it was growing, and was strong even in Parliament. All this foretold that seventeenth-century England would have plenty of troubles to face, though no such dangers from foreign foes and religious strife as had threatened it during the seventy years of Elizabeth's life and the forty-five of her reign. She died at Richmond in the seventieth year of her age in 1603.

"TOGETHER"

When Horse and Rider each can trust the
    other everywhere,
It takes a fence and more than a fence to pound
    that happy pair;
For the one will do what the other demands,
    although he is beaten and blown,
And when it is done, they can live through a
    run that neither could face alone.

When Crew and Captain understand each other
    to the core,
It takes a gale and more than a gale to put
    their ship ashore;
For the one will do what the other commands,
    although they are chilled to the bone,

And both together can live through weather
    that neither could face alone.

When King and People understand each other
    past a doubt,
It takes a foe and more than a foe to knock that
    country out;
For the one will do what the other one asks as
    soon as the need is known,
And hand in hand they can make a stand which
    neither could make alone!

This wisdom had Elizabeth and all her sub-
    jects too,
For she was theirs and they were hers as well
    the Spaniard knew;
For when his grim Armada came to conquer
    the Nation and Throne,
Why, back to back they met an attack that
    neither could face alone!

It is not wealth nor talk nor trade nor schools
    nor even the Vote,
Will save your land when the enemy's hand is
    tightening round your throat.
But a King and a People who thoroughly trust
    each other in all that is done
Can sleep on their bed without any dread —
    for the world will leave 'em alone!

CHAPTER VIII

THE EARLY STUARTS AND THE GREAT CIVIL WAR, 1603-60

HENRY VIII and Elizabeth had given England unity and patriotism. Would the next race of kings, the Stuarts, be able to maintain unity? That was the question which every one was asking while King James I was slowly riding from Scotland to London in 1603. James, of whom you may read the character in Sir Walter Scott's beautiful story, "The Fortunes of Nigel," was already thirty-five, "an old King," he said; and he had had a miserable time in Scotland between the turbulent nobles and the Presbyterian ministers who were always preaching at him. And he had been very poor. He knew England to be rich, and thought he was going to be a rich and great King. He was a firm and very learned Protestant, a kindly man, though irritable and conceited. He saw a great deal farther than most of his subjects saw, but he never understood the temper of the English people; and above all he did not know, as the

James I, 1603-25; his character.

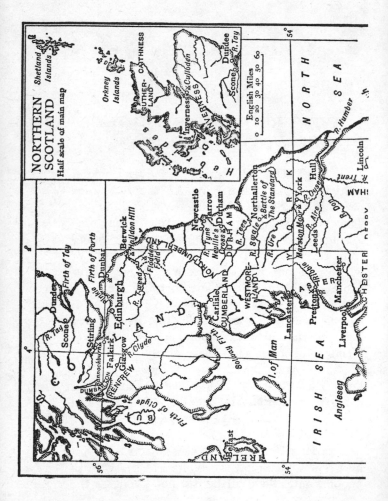

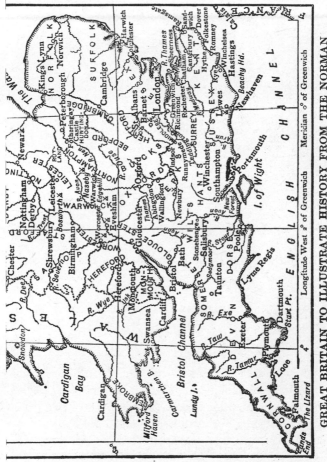

GREAT BRITAIN TO ILLUSTRATE HISTORY FROM THE NORMAN
CONQUEST TO THE PRESENT DAY

Tudors had known, when he had "come to the place called Stop." You might describe him as

The child of Mary Queen of Scots,
    A shifty mother's shiftless son,
Bred up among intrigues and plots
    Learned in all things, wise in none!
Ungainly, babbling, wasteful, weak,
    Shrewd, clever, cowardly, pedantic,
The sight of steel would blanch his cheek,
    The smell of baccy drive him frantic.
He was the author of his line —
    He wrote that witches should be burnt;
He wrote that monarchs were divine,
    And left a son who proved they weren't!

Temper of England. Now the temper of the English people was going to be a very serious matter. They were fully "grown up," and fully aware that they were grown up; and they did not want to be "in leading strings" any longer. Even the great Elizabeth, in her last years, had galled this proud temper a good deal. She had scolded her Parliaments and done high-handed things against the law. But she had served and guided her people faithfully, and they knew it and made allowances accordingly.

Mistakes of the Stuart Kings. James I and his son Charles I, never thought of themselves as "servants" of their people.

They wanted to rule as the Tudors had ruled,
though the need for the guidance and the leading strings had passed away. They were not
"tyrants" or cruel men or extortioners, but
they irritated the nation until they provoked
rebellion and civil war. And so they broke
the unity of King and People, which was hardly
restored again before the reign of Victoria the
Great.

The main thing to remember about them is
that they quarrelled continually with their
Parliaments, with the House of Lords almost
as much as with the House of Commons; and
nearly all their quarrels were over religion or
money. The House of Commons took the
lead in the quarrels, because it was the most
powerful body of gentlemen in the country.
The Tudors had flattered and strengthened it
enormously, and added very largely to its numbers; for they had been rather afraid of the
House of Lords. The Stuarts added more
than a hundred members to the House of Lords
in the hope of getting its support against the
Commons, but without much success.

First then, for the quarrels about religion.
England was growing more Puritan every day.
Men saw that the Church of Rome had "set
its house in order" since the Reformation, and
so was regaining its ground everywhere. It

Their quarrels with Parliaments.

Religious quarrels: dangers from Rome again.

was catching hold of kings and courtiers, even in lands that had been soundly Protestant fifty years before. Spain backed it up with sword and gun; and Spain, though the old men who had beaten the Armada might laugh at her, still seemed to be a gigantic power. James I was bent on keeping peace with Spain and wished his son to marry a Spanish princess. This, said the Puritans, would simply bring back the Pope and Popery to England. Once some wicked and hot-headed Catholics made a plot to blow up the King and both Houses of Parliament with gunpowder (1605). I think you have all heard of Guy Fawkes and the "Fifth of November," but perhaps, when we see his absurd figure carried about in the streets, we are apt to forget that, on that day in the year 1605, he was actually found in a cellar under the Houses of Parliament, watching a lot of barrels of gunpowder to which he was going to set light the next morning when Parliament should have met. The King and the Prince of Wales, and all the Bishops, Lords and Commons would have met a horrible death, and the friends of Fawkes would then have seized the Government on behalf of the Catholics. No wonder Protestants hated and feared a religion in whose name such things could be planned. The Puritans also said that the English Church

James's leaning to Spain.

The "Gunpowder Plot," 1605.

Growth of the Puritans; "High Church" and "Low Church."

was getting too much like the Catholic Church;
or becoming, as we should say now, too "High
Church." The bishops were too powerful, the
services too splendid, even the teaching was
growing Catholic again. So these Puritans
began to cry out, first for a limit to the power of
the bishops, then for their abolition, and finally
for the abolition of the Prayer Book. But,
when it came to that cry, England was by no
means united, and at last was divided on the
religious question into two camps of nearly
equal strength, who were obliged to fight it
out in a bloody civil war.

On the second question, the quarrels about
money, which we can call the "civil" as opposed
to the religious causes of quarrel, there was no
real division of opinions. No one of any importance in England wanted the King to be
able to take taxes at his pleasure, nor to keep
people in prison without bringing them to
trial, nor to make war or peace without consulting his Parliament. The Tudors had done
many of these things, but, on the whole, with
the approval of the whole nation and for its
good. The people they kept in prison without
trial were usually foreign spies or traitors, who
were threatening the very existence of England
as a nation. James and Charles, however, sent
members of Parliament to prison for speeches

*Civil
quarrels;
unlawful
taxation,
etc.*

made in Parliament against the "tyranny" of the bishops, against taxes, against unpatriotic alliances with Spain. They took, at the English ports, Customs' duties on goods without consent of Parliament. They did indeed maintain a fine Navy, and they certainly built splendid ships, but they did nothing with them. Their sailors were itching to cut Spanish and Popish throats far away in America, and Portuguese throats far away in India; but the fleet was kept hanging about in the Channel, while the flag was insulted by Frenchmen, by Spaniards, and even by our old friends, the Protestant Dutch. So at last men were unwilling to serve in such a Navy; and had to be "impressed," that is, compelled to serve. And when King Charles, in 1635–6–7, asked for a tax called "Ship-money," to maintain the Navy, men began to say "No," "not without consent of Parliament," and so on.

The Stuart Navy.

"Ship-money," 1637.

It was the same story with the Army, or rather with the old "militia" of "every man armed in his county," which did duty for an Army. The Tudors had not been very successful in their efforts to make this force a real one. Men hated the service and shirked it when they could; they talked nonsense about "England not wanting an Army when she had got such a fine Navy." You will often hear the same sort

The Army or "Militia."

of nonsense talked nowadays; don't believe it!
King James, toward the end of his reign, had
a fine opportunity of showing that England
could bite by land as well as by sea; for a fright- The
Thirty
Years'
War in
Ger-
many,
1618-48.
ful war broke out in Germany between Catholics
and Protestants, which was to last for thirty
years; and all good Protestants in England and
Scotland were eager to go and help their brothers in Germany. But James couldn't make his
mind up: he talked big and sent messengers
flying about to the Kings of Europe, but *act*
he would not; and so nothing was done except
that a great many volunteers went, both from
England and Scotland, and learned soldiering
to some purpose, as James's son, King Charles
I, was to find out one day. Till that day there
was no real *Army* in England, although Charles,
when he came to the throne, tried to establish
a general right of "impressing" soldiers, and
quarrelled with his Parliaments at once about
it. Lastly, James dismissed all his Parliaments
in anger, and used rude language in doing so.
When he died in 1625, nearly all the seeds of the Death of
James I,
1625.
future civil war had been sowed.

Charles I, the "Martyr King," was a very Charles I,
1625-49;
his char-
acter.
different man from his father; he was shy,
proud, cold, ignorant of the world, obstinate
and mistrustful. He did not mean to lie, but
he hardly ever told the whole truth; and so

neither his enemies nor his friends could trust
him. James would have liked to be good
friends with his people, and was at bottom
what we call "a good fellow," with a strong
sense of fun. Charles never made a joke in
his life, and did not care twopence for public
opinion, or for being friends with any one except his bishops. His wife, moreover, was a
Catholic and a Frenchwoman and cared nothing
for England. Though a firm Protestant,
Charles was much more "High Church" than
James, and wanted to give the bishops more
power. He did once interfere (1627) on behalf
of the French Protestants who were (rather
mildly) ill treated at that time by their Kings,
but he made a complete mess of the task. That
was at the beginning of his reign, and, as in
his first four years he quarrelled openly with his
first three Parliaments, he could hardly get
money enough to help him to live and govern
England, and none to defend the honour of
England abroad. Then for eleven years,
1629–40, he called no Parliament at all. This
was the longest interval without a Parliament
since the reign of Henry III, and to all Englishmen, whose tempers were now boiling over, it
seemed intolerable.

His quarrels with three Parliaments, 1625-9.

Eleven years without Parliament, 1629-40.

Prosperity of English trade.

During this period Charles took the Customs'
duties at the ports, though Parliament had

never granted them to him, and they proved
to be his main source of income, for, of course,
the long peace since 1605 had greatly increased
English trade, not only with all European countries (especially Turkey, Russia, Portugal and
Spain), but also, in spite of Spanish jealousy,
with Spanish America, the West and East
Indies, and the Colonies which were now beginning to be founded in North America (as I
will tell you later on in Chapter IX). Our "East
India Company," which began to build for us our
Indian Empire of to-day, had been founded at
the end of Elizabeth's reign.

Beside the "Customs," there were lots of other
little sources of income, many of them quite
against the law, and altogether Charles had a
revenue of about a million pounds a year, which
certainly enabled him to live as long as he could
keep the peace. Perhaps he might never have
called a Parliament again if he had not
quarrelled about religion with his subjects in
Scotland. His Archbishop of Canterbury was
William Laud, an honourable but narrow-
minded man, who set himself to weed out the
Puritan party in the Church of England, and to
make every one conform to the services of the
Prayer Book. All Puritan England was already growling deeply at this, when it occurred
to Laud to try to enforce the same services and

Charles's
quarrel
with
Scotland,
1637.

ceremonies on Presbyterian Scotland. Some steps in this direction had been begun by King James, but had met with very little success; there were, however, already some sort of restored bishops in Scotland, though they had no power. Suddenly, in 1637, Charles resolved to force upon Scotland the whole of the Prayer Book, as a first step toward making the Church quite uniform in the two kingdoms.

Resistance of the Scots, 1638. Scotland, poor, proud, and intensely patriotic, had for long felt sore and neglected since its native kings had gone from Edinburgh to London. At this "English" insult it simply rose and slammed the door in the faces of the King and his Archbishop. A "Covenant" was signed in Edinburgh and all over Scotland, which bound all men by the most solemn oath to maintain the Presbyterian Church and to root out bishops and all their works; the Covenanters flatly refused all compromise, and Charles, if he were to remain a king at all in Scotland, would have to fight. It would be no easy task; for neither Edward I nor Henry VIII at the head of a united England had been successful against the Scots. And Charles and Laud were almost the only people in England who did not think the Scots were right to resist! The Scots got together a much better army than Charles could get, and faced him sturdily;

The "Covenant," 1638.

the first "Bishops' War," as the Puritans called it, was a dead failure. "Call your Parliament, Sir," was the only advice his councillors could give the King. The first 'Bishops' War," 1639.

Charles gave way, and, in April, 1640, called a Parliament which, as he dismissed it in a few days, had the nickname of "The Short Parliament." For, instead of giving him cash to crush Scotland with, it began to pour out a torrent of the grievances of the past eleven years, nay, of the past thirty-seven years; grievances about taxes, customs, ship-money; about bishops, popery in high places, judges who twisted the law to please the King, and so forth. After one more effort at war with Scotland in the summer, during which the Scots simply walked into England as far as Durham and sat down there, the King had to own himself beaten, and to call, on November 3, 1640, a Parliament that was to be anything but short. History knows it as "The Long Parliament." The Short Parliament, April-May, 1640.

The second "Bishops' War," 1640.

Meeting of the Long Parliament, Nov. 3, 1640.

The leaders of this body were no revolutionists or "radicals." Nearly all were great lawyers or country gentlemen of old families and rich estates: Hampden, Pym, Holles, Vane, Cromwell, Hyde, Falkland, were the leaders in the Commons; Essex, Warwick, Bedford, Broke, and Saye in the Lords. The great merchants of the City of London, which was already perhaps the greatest place of trade in the world, were on the same side.

No one had the least intention of upsetting the throne of King Charles. But in civil matters all were agreed in wishing to purify the Law Courts and to restore the "ancient constitution," by which they meant the control of Parliament over the Crown, as it had existed before the Wars of the Roses. The "strong government" of the Tudors, they said, had been necessary at the time; it was no longer necessary. The King of England ought to be a "limited monarch," not an "absolute monarch," and Charles must be made to realize the fact.

So, in about nine months, the whole fabric of the civil government was thoroughly overhauled. The King's one honourable and clever minister, the Earl of Strafford, was sent to the Tower and at length beheaded. Archbishop Laud was sent to the Tower. The judges who had twisted the law to please the King were removed, and provision was made against their twisting it in the future. Several new law courts, which had grown up in Tudor times, were taken away: the power of levying any taxes without full consent of Parliament was taken away; and it was decided that henceforward Parliament should meet at least every three years.

All this was done with the most thundering applause of the nation, from Tweed to Tamar, from Kent to Cumberland; for, as I have said, all men were agreed as to the "civil" causes of complaint against their King. But it was another story when questions relating to religion were touched. Only one half of England was Puritan or wished to abolish bishops or Prayer Book. Three fourths of the House of Lords and nearly half the House of Commons were against making any such change; and this at once began to give the King "a party" in the State. He meant to use that party not only to save the Church, but also, if possible, to restore his own "strong government" in civil matters. So things stood in the autumn of 1641; and two events then hurried on the civil war, the King's visit to Scotland, and a rebellion in Ireland.

Our Parliament men easily guessed that the King's visit to Scotland was made in order to see whether, if he had to fight his Parliament, the Scots would help him. For he gave the Scots everything that they asked, and showered honours on their leaders; in fact, he appealed to their old jealousy of England. Still he got little or no promise of help there.

To understand the other thing, the Irish rebellion, we must go back a long way. No

A rift in the Nation.

The religious question.

The King's visit to Scotland, August, 1641.

The Irish Rebellion October, 1641.

English sovereign had seriously tried to *govern*
Ireland before the Tudors. The kings had
often made grants of Irish land to Englishmen,
who had then gone over there and had, in a few
years, become wilder than the Irish themselves.
There was some shadow of English government
in Leinster, with a "Lord Deputy" as Governor,
and a sort of Irish Parliament; but, in the fifteenth century, the English territory had shrunk
to a very narrow district round Dublin called
"the Pale." Outside the Pale, it was all
broken heads and stolen cows, as it had been
for a thousand years. But Henry VIII had
taken the task of government in hand, and had
tried to turn the wild Irish chiefs into decent
English landowners, who should really come to
Parliament, help the judges in keeping order,
and cultivate their lands properly. He had
dissolved the Irish monasteries as he had dissolved the English, and had given their lands
to these chiefs. He put down rebellious earls
with a very strong hand, and quite successfully.
He had taken the title of "King" of Ireland.
The "Reformation" had been started in Ireland under Edward VI, but there had been little
Reformation for Mary to suppress, and no
"heretics" were burned there. Certainly, until
the middle of the sixteenth century, Ireland
had shown little affection for Pope or Catholic

IRELAND

English Miles
0 20 30 40 60

ULSTER

Londonderry

Belfast

CONNAUGHT

x R. Boyne
THE PALE
in the 15th. Century
Dublin

LEINSTER

Limerick

MUNSTER

Waterford

Emery Walker sc.

faith. But rebellion in some shape remained Catholic rebellions the one thing that Irish chiefs loved, and it occurred to some of them, especially to one Shan O'Neill, early in the reign of Elizabeth, that *a rebellion in the name of religion* would be a much more successful affair than without that name: "England is now Protestant; therefore let Ireland rise for the Pope," was Shan's idea. Philip of Spain saw a splendid chance (for the Pope and himself) of injuring Elizabeth by sending aid to Irish-Catholic with Spanish aid. rebellions; and, from 1570 at least, he continued to do so either secretly or openly until his death. The idea "caught on," as we should say, with the whole Irish nation, and every one went about shouting "Pope aboo," "Spain aboo," and "O'Neil (or Desmond, or some other wild earl) aboo." Thus England, when she tried to keep order, always appeared to be "persecuting" Catholics in Ireland. But Colonies or "Plantations" in Ireland in sixteenth century. Elizabeth could not face the frightful cost of keeping order there until the last two years of her reign, when she went to work in earnest and with some success. Usually she had preferred to plant "colonies" of Englishmen upon some Irish districts which had been confiscated after a rebellion. So Munster was "planted," 1583; so Ulster was planted with Scottish land- Colony of Ulster 1607. owners, tradesmen and artisans by James I.

These last were mostly Presbyterians, and made vigorous and successful colonists. But, of course, the Irish landowners, who had rebelled and been turned out, always hoped to recover their land. And the rebellion of 1641 was prompted either by this hope, or by the fear of fresh confiscation.

Rebellion of Catholics, 1641.

But to the Puritans in the English Parliament it seemed to be simply a rebellion of the "wicked Papists," "probably got up by the King," they said, "certainly by the Queen, in order to give excuse for raising an army to use against the English Parliament." And,

English Parliament frightened.

with this fear in their heads, the leaders of Parliament were now driven to take steps far beyond any they had intended a year before.

The "Militia Bill," December, 1641.

First they brought forward laws for the utter abolition of bishops and all their works; and then laws to transfer the command of the army or militia from the Crown to Parliament.

Civil War in sight.

This last was revolution pure and simple. No king could agree to this, and so Charles began to set about preparations for war. Large numbers of Members of Parliament came to join him from both houses; but those that remained at Westminster were of course all the more determined to fight.

Cavaliers and Roundheads.

The words "rebellion," "treason," "traitor" are very ugly words; and traitors in those days

were put to a very ugly death. So, many
moderate men, who had hated Charles's unlawful government, and applauded all the work of
this Parliament during its first nine months,
now threw in their lot with the Crown. So
did many men who cared nothing for bishops;
Charles was their King, and his flag was flying
in the field. There were many men, too, who
hated the long sermons and the gloomy nature
of the Puritans; for the Puritans objected to
country sports, may-poles, dancing, and to
lots of innocent amusements. These "Cavaliers" called the Parliament men "Roundheads," "crop-eared rogues," and so on; they
gave the King an excellent force of cavalry,
in which arm the Parliament was at first
weak. The King's foot-soldiers were mostly
Cornishmen or Welshmen, good fellows to
fight, too.

But the Parliament had the richer districts
of the kingdom, the South and East; London
was in its grip; it had the most of the fleet;
and much the fuller purse. It is a great mistake to imagine that the war was one of gentlemen against merchants and traders. Nearly
half the country gentlemen of England were
Puritans, and at first all the leaders on both
sides were drawn from the upper classes; later
on there were one or two instances, on each side,

where men of lesser birth rose to high commands in the armies.

The equipment of each force was much the same; the infantry carried either long clumsy muskets which could shoot about 300 yards at extreme range, or "pikes," which were straight two-edged knives fastened on to long poles. Each side cast a few light field-guns, which did little damage; but later on the Parliament cast some heavy siege-guns which really finished the war. Each side had soldiers who had fought in the German wars. Prince Rupert, Sir Jacob Astley, Sir Ralph Hopton for the King; Lord Essex, Lord Manchester, Sir William Waller, Sir Thomas Fairfax for the Parliament. The King had perhaps this advantage: when the war began no one had yet dreamed of deposing him, much less of killing him. "Whatever we do, he will still be the King and his sons after him," was the idea in the minds even of the staunchest of his enemies. So at first Parliament was "afraid of beating the King too much." But Charles had no need to be afraid of beating his rebels too much.

Once battle was joined, each side displayed the greatest gallantry, chivalry and mercy. No war was ever fought with so much bloodshed *in* battle and so little cruelty *after* battle.

Except where actual fighting or a siege was going on, civil life was not interrupted. Down to the end of 1643 the advantage was on the whole with the King. Then both men and money began to fail him, and an incomparable leader came to the front for the Parliament in the person of Oliver Cromwell, who was to finish the war and die, ten years later, something very like King of Great Britain.

With what feelings the men in either army must have looked upon each other before the first great battle!

> Naked and gray the Cotswolds stand
>   Beneath the autumn sun,
> And the stubble fields on either hand
>   Where Stour and Avon run,
> There is no change in the patient land
>   That has bred us every one.
>
> She should have passed in cloud and fire
>   And saved us from this sin
> Of war — red war — 'twixt child and sire,
>   Household and kith and kin,
> In the heart of a sleepy Midland shire,
>   With the harvest scarcely in.
>
> But there is no change as we meet at last
>   On the brow-head or the plain,

Before Edgehill fight, October, 1642.

And the raw astonished ranks stand fast
   To slay or to be slain
By the men they knew in the kindly past
   That shall never come again —

By the men they met at dance or chase,
   In the tavern or the hall,
At the justice-bench and the market-place,
   At the cudgel-play or brawl,
Of their own blood and speech and race,
   Comrades or neighbours all!

More bitter than death this day must prove
   Whichever way it go,
For the brothers of the maids we love
   Make ready to lay low
Their sisters' sweethearts, as we move
   Against our dearest foe.

Thank Heaven!   At last the trumpets peal
   Before our strength gives way.
For King or for the Commonweal —
   No matter which they say,
The first dry rattle of new-drawn steel
   Changes the world to-day!

Progress of the war, 1642-3.   The King very nearly got into London, after a fierce drawn battle at Edgehill in Warwickshire, in the autumn of 1642; but the Londoners turned out in such force for the defence of the city, and looked so grim, that Charles dared not fight his way in. He fell back on Oxford, and fixed his headquarters there; it was an excellent centre; he meant to move one army up from Yorkshire, another from Cornwall, and a third from Oxford, and so to crush Parliament between three fires. All 1643 he strove for this, and his generals won victories both in the north and west. But then John Pym, the statesman who took the lead in Parliament, called in the aid of the Scots. The Scots agreed to come, but demanded that their "Covenant," to enforce the Presbyterian Church on all three kingdoms, should be the price of their coming. In 1644 they came and helped to rout the King's best army at Marston Moor, near York.

The real victor in that battle was, however, Oliver Cromwell, a Huntingdonshire squire, forty-three years of age, who had never seen a shot fired until he began to raise the sturdy Puritan farmers of the Eastern Counties for the Parliament. He trained them and led them till they became the "Ironsides," the finest cavalry in the world. Look well at them, and think of them; for they are the direct forerunners of the cavalry regiments of our present gallant little army. Cromwell was no narrow-

The King at Oxford, 1643-6.

John Pym calls in the Scots to help Parliament.

Battle of Marston Moor, 1644.

Oliver Cromwell.

The Ironsides.

minded Puritan, and for *forms* of Church government he cared not a straw. But he held that God spoke to each individual man's soul and pointed out his path for him. He thought that all forms were just so many fetters on men's souls, and that all churches, especially the Roman and English, had laid on such fetters. And he had been a strong opponent of the King in civil matters also. Moreover, he saw, as no one else saw, that "half-measures" would never finish the war. "If I met the King in the field, I would pistol him," he said.

The "New Model" Army, 1645.

In 1645 a new Parliamentary army, better paid and better armed and more in earnest, was raised under Fairfax and Cromwell, and it won, within three months, the great victory of Naseby, which practically brought the Royalist cause to an end. A few gallant Highlanders under Montrose made a diversion for the King in Scotland, but Montrose too was beaten before the year was over. Charles had already called into England all the soldiers whom he had sent to put down the Irish rebels, and he tried to get the help of these same rebels themselves. This, as you can imagine, did not make his cause more popular with his English Protestant subjects. He was in fact a very bad leader of a very good cause. Early in 1646 the King fled to the Scottish army and Oxford surren-

Battle of Naseby, 1645.

dered. The Scots, after trying to induce him to take the oath of the Covenant, sold him for £400,000 to the English Parliament as a prisoner and went back home. The Parliament spent the years 1647 and 1648 in trying to make some sort of treaty with Charles so that the government of the country might continue under a king; Charles argued each point, and was ready to promise, now this, now that, but never anything sincerely. All the time he was trying to get help from France, or from Scotland, or from Ireland

The King flies to the Scots, 1646, and is sold to the Parliament.

Meanwhile the Parliamentary leaders had to try to fulfil their treaty with the Scots. They could abolish bishops, sell all the lands of the Church of England, turn out all the Royalist parsons, and forbid the use of the Prayer Book; but they found it almost impossible to establish a Presbyterian Church in England. In reality few Englishmen wanted this. Even those who had most wanted to pull down bishops began to see that "ministers and elders" might try to force men's consciences quite as much as bishops had done. No one felt this more than Cromwell; and, what Cromwell thought, his Army, which had finished the war, thought also. This Army began to growl against its masters the Parliament. It also began to growl for the punishment of "Charles Stuart,

Parliament perplexed, 1646-7-8.

Cromwell's army quarrels with Parliament, 1647-8.

that man of blood." When Charles did at
last persuade the Scots, who were by this time
very cross with the Parliament, to come in
again on his behalf, this growl became an
open cry; the Army duly went and smashed
the Scots at Preston, and then came back to
London resolved on the King's death.

Battle of Preston, 1648.

Cromwell hesitated long; he was a merciful
man, and he saw what a terrible thing he had
to do — to kill a King! But he believed that
the Lord guided his mind, and that there
could be no peace while Charles lived. Parliament was utterly horrified at this suggestion,
but it was at the mercy of the Army which it
had created. Cromwell turned out over a
hundred of its most moderate members and
terrified the remainder. A sham court of justice was established to try and to condemn
the King. Charles, of course, refused to acknowledge that any court had any power to try
him; and he met his death on January 30, 1649,
with perfect serenity and courage. The very
men who did the deed were terrified at what
they were doing.

Trial and Death of Charles I, January 30, 1649.

Charles was a martyr, a martyr for the English Church and its government by bishops,
a martyr for our beautiful and dear Prayer
Book. But the fact that he was a martyr did
not make him a good king or a good man.

Was Charles a martyr?

Yet, though Charles had often overridden the law, and, if he had got back to power, would have done so again, what had the Army and the dregs of the Long Parliament to put in his place? They confiscated and sold to new owners much of the land of those who had fought for the King. They set up a sort of Republic which they called "The Commonwealth," with a Council of State, and a single House of Parliament, in fact the "Rump" of the Long Parliament, as witty cavaliers called it. They abolished the House of Lords the day after they had murdered the King. In reality they had abolished Law, Order, and the old *natural* Constitution; and all their efforts for the next eleven years to put anything *artificial* in its place were hopeless failures. The one real FACT left in England was the Army; this meant the rule of the Sword, the worst of all conceivable tyrannies, however good the men may be who wield that Sword.

They were good men who wielded it. Cromwell was a man of the most lofty character, and so were many of his associates. They were also great patriots and great Englishmen. But nineteen twentieths of Englishmen hated the whole thing heart and soul, looked upon Charles I's death as an abominable murder, and only prayed for Charles II to come and avenge it.

What is to be put in his place?

The "Commonwealth" or Republic.

The Rule of the Sword.

Charles II in exile and in Scotland.

That young man, now nineteen years old, had fled to the Continent. The Scots invited him to Scotland, made him take the Covenant (which he hated), and prepared to fight for him.

Cromwell in Ireland, 1649.

But Cromwell and his Ironsides, after going across and stamping out the Irish rebellion with a great deal of cruelty, made short work of one Scottish army at Dunbar in 1650, and of an-

Battles of Dunbar, 1650, and Worcester, 1651.

other, which had invaded England, at Worcester in 1651. The young King fought most gallantly at the latter battle, and had a series of hair-breadth escapes before he regained the Continent; you have often heard, perhaps, of how he spent a day in hiding in the upper branches of a great oak tree in Shropshire —

> While far below the Roundhead rode
> And hummed a surly hymn.

That is why people wear oak 'eaves on May 29, and why so many public houses still bear the sign of the "Royal Oak."

Yet, if civil war was over, there was no civil

Cromwell "Lord Protector" of England, Scotland, and Ireland, 1653-8.

peace in Britain; and in 1653 Cromwell was obliged to turn out the "Rump" of the Long Parliament and to take on himself the government of England, Scotland, and Ireland as "Protector," a title which pleased his old friends little more than it pleased his old enemies.

He made experiment after experiment in forms
of government; tried sometimes with, and
sometimes without, some sort of sham Parliament; once he even tried to create a sort of
sham House of Lords. But all these things
were only thin disguises for the rule of the
Sword and the Army. He was much pressed
to take the title of king and to restore the old His rule good but hated.
Constitution, but from this he shrank. Except
to Papists and to the beaten Church of England
he was not intolerant; he believed in letting
men's consciences be free, and he strove to
make people righteous and God-fearing. All
that, however, was a dismal failure; it only
disgusted all moderate people with the whole
Puritan creed.

Yet, in Oliver's five years of rule, he accom- His Parliament of the three kingdoms.
plished what the Stuarts had not done in forty-
five. Not only had he subdued Scotland and
Ireland, but he even made them send thirty
members apiece to a sort of united Parliament
in England. And far more than this: he made
the name of England once more dreaded and
honoured abroad as it had not been since the
death of Elizabeth. He wrung from the Dutch His care of the Navy.
a heavy payment for some wrongs they had
done our traders in the Far East; he won for
us a share in that Far-Eastern trade. He fell
upon the Spaniards in the true style of Drake

and Raleigh; he took their great plate fleet; he tore Jamaica from them; he sent his Ironsides to France to aid France against Spain; they were the first great English army seen abroad since the fifteenth century, and where they fought they swept all before them. He took up the great cause of Protestantism all over Europe When he died in 1658 England was again the first naval power and almost the first military power in the world.

His victories over Spain.

His death, 1658.

But when his son Richard ("lazy Dick" or "tumbledown Dick," as people called him) succeeded him as Protector, the whole unnatural arrangement crumbled away at once, because it did not suit the spirit of the English people. There were eighteen months of anarchy; now some soldier, now the restored "Rump," held power. At last, in January, 1660, General Monck, an old soldier of Cromwell's, who had the command in Scotland, made up his mind to restore the exiled King, Charles II.

Richard Cromwell, Protector, 1658-9.

Anarchy.

And on his thirtieth birthday, the 29th of May, 1660, that clever and unprincipled young gentleman rode into London amid the tears and shouts of a people gone mad with joy. The reign of the Sword was over, the reign of the Law had begun. Unfortunately this reign of the Sword left on men's minds an unreasonable hatred and fear, not only of this Puritan

Restoration of King Charles II, May 29, 1660.

army, but of all armies and that hatred and fear have too often paralyzed the arm of England, and is not wholly dead to-day. It has prevented men from seeing that to serve King and country in the Army is the second best profession for Englishmen of all classes; to serve in the Navy, I suppose all admit, is the best. Charles II prudently kept up a few of the regiments of Cromwell's old army, and even increased it a little during his reign. But he had often hard work to pay it, for his Parliaments were always jealous of a power that they knew had been their master once and might be so again.

CHAPTER IX

THE FALL OF THE STUARTS AND THE REVOLUTION, 1660–1688

Charles II, 1660-85.

Again a changed England.

THE lessons of the "Great Rebellion" were by no means thrown away upon Charles II. No king after 1660 ever attempted to raise a penny without consent of Parliament. Once, but only once, at the end of his reign, Charles let four years go by without calling a Parliament. Once, but only for a moment, an unlawful court of justice was created by James II; and there were hardly any other attempts at "strong government" of the Tudor type. There were plenty of quarrels to come between kings and parliaments, but these were nearly always about religion or foreign wars.

The Church restored.

As far as possible everything was restored in Great Britain and Ireland as it had existed just before the Civil War. The two houses of Parliament, with all their old power, were restored. The Church of England, with Prayer Book and bishops, was restored as in 1640. It had suffered quite as much as the Crown,

or the Cavaliers who had fought for the Crown.
A certain amount but by no means all of the
land was restored to its rightful owners. The
church livings had been almost all given away
to Presbyterians and other Dissenters. During
the Rebellion a whole crop of "sects" had arisen,
some of which, like the Congregationalists,
Baptists, and Quakers, are still with us. In
1660 all wished for nothing better than a peaceful life, and to conduct their worship in their
own way. No one could complain when the
church livings were given back to the Church
of England; but it was a great mistake of
Parliament and Church to prevent the Dissenters from holding their public worship as
they pleased. It was a lasting misfortune for
England that a series of laws was passed in the
reign of Charles II to shut out both Catholics
and Protestant Dissenters from all offices in
the State, and even from offices in town councils.
Catholics were excluded from Parliament, for
the Great Rebellion had left a hatred of popery
greater than that which had existed before it.
These intolerant laws, though partly softened
for Protestant Dissenters in 1690, and for
Catholics also in the reign of George III, were
not abolished till 1828 and 1829. Of course,
no persons now suffered death for their religion
(and it was in Charles II's reign that Queen

The Dissenters.

Parliament passes laws against Dissenters, 1661-5.

Mary's laws for burning heretics were finally wiped out), but many Dissenters were imprisoned, among them John Bunyan, author of "Pilgrim's Progress."

The Restoration in Scotland.

In Scotland a similar restoration took place of the old Scottish Parliament, in which Lords and Commons had always sat in one house; of Church government by bishops; of lands which had been confiscated. The extreme Covenanters refused to recognize these changes, and before long broke out into open rebellion in the south-west. Rebellion went on smouldering a good deal until 1688; much cruelty was exercised, and much more was wrongly believed to have been exercised in putting it down. Charles's English ministers would have liked to govern Scotland from London and to unite the two Parliaments, but the patriotic spirit of the smaller country was as yet entirely against this.

Character of Charles II.

King Charles II came back to find a new kind of England, an England less high-minded, less romantic, more "modern," and more commonplace than before the war. The country was again set upon peace, order, and money-getting. The King set a bad example in his private life, but in his public life he was not by any means a bad King. He was very clever, and had a keen eye for the interests of trade,

of the Colonies, and of the Navy. The Crom-
wellians had bequeathed to him a very fine
Navy; but too often he let it rot for want of
spending money on it. His sailors were badly
paid and badly cared for; he let his contractors
swindle him, and he was too idle to look into
small but important matters himself. Also
he was always shockingly in want of money to
spend upon pleasure, and, if Parliament would
not give him enough, he was apt to ask the
King of France to pay him large sums, in return
for which he would promise to do something
which that King wanted — not always to the
honour of England. But, when he had got the
money, Charles very seldom kept his promises
to King Louis.

France was now taking the place in the eyes
of Englishmen which Spain had held in the
period 1560–1640, the place, that is, of the
national bugbear and terror, whose vast army
and vast wealth were to be used to help the
Pope and to spread the Catholic faith. Englishmen wanted to fight King Louis, just as they
had wanted to fight King Philip in James I's
days. Charles II, however, saw that our real
rivals were the Protestant Dutch, whose merchant-ships covered all seas, whose trading
stations were all over the world. And, if
you are to understand this, it is time that I

Englishmen's dread of France,

and rivalry with the Dutch.

told you something about the growth of our own Colonial Empire.

The idea of Colonies beyond the Seas.

The first idea of all voyages to distant countries had been to get either gold and silver, or precious goods like silk and spices, which could not be grown in Europe. Spain, Portugal, Holland, and France had all been ahead of us in the race of discovery; but we were going to beat them all in the long run. It was Sir

Sir Walter Raleigh.

Walter Raleigh, in Elizabeth's reign, who first imagined a true "colony." He did not mean, as the Spaniards meant, a sort of shop, in which Englishmen were to buy gold or silk or spices; but rather a "plantation" of Englishmen in some distant land who were to buy all their goods, their iron tools, their woollen clothes, their linen and their boots from England. This would, in the first place, give an enormous lift to English manufacturers, and, in the second place, would create a piece of "England-beyond-the-sea," a piece, in fact, of an English *Empire*. Raleigh planned to plant such a colony in Virginia, on the shore of North America; it collapsed for want of funds. But the idea lived on, and in 1606 it was taken up again by a group of London merchants, who subscribed money and sent out colonists. By the year 1620 Virginia was a flourishing little state.

In that year some sturdy Puritans, since called

the "Pilgrim Fathers," got leave to emigrate to North America. They objected to being compelled to use the Prayer Book service in England, and wanted to worship God in their own fashion; and they founded a little state called "Plymouth" on the American coast. Other colonies, some religious, some commercial in their origin, soon followed, and by 1660 the whole eastern coast of North America was dotted with little English states; but between Virginia and the more sternly Puritan "New England" lay a little wedge on the valley of the River Hudson, which had been settled by the Dutch. There was no gold in North America, and, except tobacco, no rich natural crop; but there was a virgin soil of great fertility, vast forests full of valuable timber, swarms of fur-bearing animals like beavers, and splendid fisheries on the coasts. So these peoples rapidly grew into rich and prosperous little states, working, in a climate not unlike that of Europe, at the same sort of work that their fathers had known across the ocean.

But many of the Colonies were full of Puritans and Protestant Dissenters, the very men who, in King Charles I's reign, had fought against the Crown. So there was born, in all our colonists, a spirit of resistance to government in general, and the quite foolish notion that all

The Pilgrim Fathers in America, 1620.

British America in seventeenth century

Temper of the Colonists.

government is oppressive. Such a spirit might easily lead to rebellion. The colonists, however, knew well that all round them were Frenchmen, Dutchmen, and Spaniards, casting greedy eyes on their riches, and that against these foes only the English fleet could protect them. So some sort of pretence of loyalty to their Mother Country was for many years almost a necessity to them. The Mother Country usually left them to themselves; it never taxed them; it sent them Governors, who hoisted a British flag outside their houses, and "took the lead in Society," but did little other governing. Each colony set up a miniature House of Commons, or something like it, of its own, and made its own laws on the English model. On one thing only England insisted, that the colonists were to buy their goods wholly from English merchants; and if they produced any goods which England wanted and could not grow herself (*e. g.*, tobacco, rice, beaver skins) they were to send all such goods to England.

Charles II fought two great wars with the Dutch during his reign; and great sailors came to the front, though none as great as Robert Blake, who had been Cromwell's admiral. The sailors and the Navy covered themselves with glory, but, as I said above, the management of the service was shockingly bad, and

Government of the Colonies.

The two Dutch Wars, 1664 and 1672.

it was no thanks to King Charles that the Dutch
did not win.

THE DUTCH IN THE MEDWAY

If war were won by feasting,
  Or victory by song,
Or safety found in sleeping sound,
  How England would be strong!
But honour and dominion
  Are not maintainéd so,
They're only got by sword and shot,
  And this the Dutchmen know!

The moneys that should feed us
  You spend on your delight;
How can you then have sailor-men
  To aid you in your fight?
Our fish and cheese are rotten,
  Which makes the scurvy grow —
We cannot serve you if we starve,
  And this the Dutchmen know!

Our ships in every harbour
  Be neither whole nor sound,
And, when we seek to mend a leak,
  No oakum can be found,
Or, if it is, the caulkers,
  And carpenters also,
For lack of pay, have gone away,
  And this the Dutchmen know!

Mere powder, guns, and bullets
   We scarce can get at all,
Their price was spent in merriment
   And revel at Whitehall,
While we in tattered doublets,
   From ship to ship must row,
Beseeching friends for odds and ends —
   And this the Dutchmen know!

No king will heed our warnings,
   No Court will pay our claims —
Our King and Court for their disport
   Do sell the very Thames!
For, now De Ruyter's topsails
   Off naked Chatham show,
We dare not meet him with our fleet —
   And this the Dutchmen know!

There were some fearful drawn battles, both in the North Sea and the Channel. Once the Dutch sailed into the Thames and the Medway and burned a lot of our ships at Chatham. But the main result of these wars was that the Dutch gave up to us their colony in North America, New York. which was henceforth to be called New York. In the same reign "North and South Carolina" were added to our American list of states; they lie south of Virginia, are hot and swampy, and produce mainly rice and tobacco.

Other Colonies. Besides these Colonies we possessed several valuable West Indian Islands, notably Jamaica,

which grew sugar; we had a whale-fishing and
fur-trading station in Hudson's Bay, northward from the French settlements in Canada;
we had several little dots of land protected
by forts on the west coast of Africa, whence
we imported black slaves to our own and the
Spanish colonies; and, in India, we had Bombay
and Madras. The "East India Company"
had been founded to trade with the Far East
(from which the Dutch had steadily driven out
the first European traders, the Portuguese),
as far back as the end of Elizabeth's reign.
Dutch, Frenchmen, and Englishmen scrambled
against each other to get permission, from the
"Great Moguls" and other Eastern Kings with
magnificent names, to sell and buy in those
countries; and, on the whole, during the seventeenth century the English company got the
best of trade with Hindostan into its hands.
So you see the seeds of a great empire were
already sown, and the colonial trade made
English merchants both rich and very adventurous.

I wish I could say as much good for Charles
II's reign at home as abroad, but I cannot.
And this is mainly because in his reign we feel
that England had ceased to be united, and
seemed to have little chance of recovering its
unity. The notion that "all Kings are trying

Parties in
Parlia-
ment.

to oppress all peoples," seems to have grown up; it was the outcome of the Civil War. So there are now two "parties" in Parliament and even in the nation. There are the party of the King and his ministers and the party of those who are not his ministers, but would like to be. These parties were then called "Tories" and "Whigs;" in our days they call themselves "Conservatives" and "Liberals" (or "Radicals"). Each was supposed to represent certain principles of government; the Tories were for Church and Crown and gentlemen; the Whigs for dissenters, for trade, and for all who would bully the King.

"Whig" and "Tory."

Tories were supposed to be against all changes in laws or institutions; the Whigs were supposed to favour moderate and slow changes of law. Both professed to be utterly loyal to the Constitution—*i.e.*, to government by King, Lords, and Commons. But neither was really true to its original principles. The Whigs originally favoured a vast empire, and the careful protection of British trade, by war if necessary, especially by war with Catholic France, whereas the Tories were all for a French alliance and despised trade and colonies. Nowadays things have reversed themselves; and it is the Conservatives (or Tories) who want to protect British trade, to keep a large Army and

Their pretended principles.

Navy always ready for war, and to win the love of our brothers in the Colonies. Each party has constantly taken a different view of what the exact needs of Britain are, and each has exaggerated its own view, out of rivalry with the other party.

And this has been unfortunate; for it has too often made the leaders of each party tell lies to the people of Great Britain, in order to get their friends elected to Parliament, and themselves to office as the King's ministers. For you will see, if you reflect, that, when every law and every grant of money has to be passed by both houses of Parliament, it would be of no use to a king to have Whig ministers if there was a Tory majority in the House of Commons; a king who wanted to govern well and without quarrels *must* take ministers from the party which, for the time, has the upper hand in the House of Commons. In those days the House of Commons was chosen by a very small body of electors; now it is chosen by almost all the grown-up men in Great Britain. But the principle was the same then as now; a king who, perhaps, wanted to make a "Whig" war or carry a "Whig" law might suddenly find himself, after the election of a new Parliament, face to face with a "Tory" House of Commons, and so he would have to dismiss his Whig ministers, take Tory ministers, and drop his "Whig" war or his "Whig" law. No doubt it has made kings govern according to what was supposed to be the wish of their people for the time being; but, in the first place, a people as a whole seldom wishes the same thing for many years on end, and does not by any means always wish what is best for the country; in the second place, the system leads to friction and quarrel between parties, and so to *waste of power* and lack of union in the nation.

Question of the Succession.

All this was only beginning in Charles II's reign, but it was beginning, and it was going to go on and get worse. It has gone on and got worse every day until now. In Charles II's time Parliament was constantly the scene of fierce party disputes, mainly upon religion. Charles had no lawful sons, and his heir was his brother James, who after the death of his first wife had become a Catholic and married an Italian Catholic lady; Charles himself was accused of favouring Catholics, even of being secretly a Catholic. Wild stories were started and believed of "Popish plots" to kill Charles and set up James. (Charles, who was perhaps the most genuinely humorous of all our kings, said to his brother, "Dear James, no one would be such a fool as to kill me in order to make you King.") The Whigs got up a plan to shut out

The "Popish Plot," 1678.

James from the succession and to set up a bastard son of Charles in his place; in 1680-1681 it looked almost like a civil war between Tories and Whigs. But all moderate men dreaded this, and the King played his game so cleverly that, when he died in 1685, his brother James succeeded him without trouble. Charles had taken sharp vengeance on some of the Whig plotters, and their families did not forget the fact. *Death of Charles II, 1685.*

James II, however, was not merely the Catholic King of a strongly Protestant people, but he was also the most obstinate man in England. If not, like Edward II, a crowned ass, he was at least a crowned mule. In three years he had wrecked his own throne, and very nearly pulled down the ancient monarchy of England on the top of himself. His Parliament was quite loyal and quite prepared to shut its eyes to his Catholic faith, if he would not flaunt it in every one's face. But, from the very first, he set himself not only to do this, but to make the Catholics supreme in the State. He wished to give them all posts in Army, Navy and Civil Service, and even in the Church of England. He thought that by promising to abolish all laws against the Protestant Dissenters he might get them to help him to abolish the laws against the Catholics also. *James II, 1658-8; his character.* *His Catholic faith.* *He tries to beguile the Dissenters 1687*

But the Dissenters, who certainly had never loved the Church of England, feared a Catholic king much more, and altogether refused to listen to James; they threw in their lot with those very churchmen and bishops who had bullied them. In Ireland, James appealed to the wildest passions of the Irish against the Protestant colonies of Englishmen which had been planted there by Elizabeth, by James I and by Cromwell, and who had been confirmed in their lands by Charles II. To the one person who *could* perhaps have helped him to put down England by the sword — namely, King Louis of France — this crowned mule turned a deaf ear, and professed that he wanted no such help. In short, he listened to nobody but a few Catholic priests in his own household.

Question of the Succession.

Until 1688 his heir had been his eldest daughter, the good and beloved Princess Mary, who had been married in 1677 to her Dutch cousin, Prince William of Orange, who was now the leader of Protestant Europe against the King of France. Most Englishmen were content to wait till James should die; then this darling Protestant girl would be their queen.

Birth of Prince James Edward, 1688.

But in June, 1688, James had a son born to him, who would, of course, be brought up as a Papist. The whole nation shivered at the prospect; its leaders, Whig and moderate

Tory alike, would wait no longer, and a secret message was at once despatched to Prince William begging him to come over to England, either to turn out King James or to teach him by force (for nothing but force would ever convince such a character) to govern better.

Prince William of Orange was the son of Charles I's daughter Mary. He was a frail little creature, nearly always ill, with an enormous hook-nose and cold gray eyes, which only lighted up in battle. His manners were also cold and unkind; but underneath all he had a soul of fire. He cared for but one thing on earth, to smash King Louis of France. He saw that rich England had been, since Cromwell's time, too much the ally of France, too much the enemy of Holland. He thought she had played false to Protestantism. If he came to England to deliver it from King James, he meant afterward to throw the whole weight and wealth of England into the alliances which he was forever knitting together against his hated enemy, France. For English "politics" and the English Constitution, for the squabble of Whigs and Tories in the English Parliament, he cared nothing at all. But he was the husband of the heiress of England, and here was his chance of power.

Men went about saying that the child just

Landing of William, 1688. born to King James was not his son at all, was no true Prince of Wales, "he had been smuggled into the Palace in a warming pan" — and much other nonsense of that sort. It suited William to believe this, or to pretend to believe it. James was well warned of what was coming, but he shut his ears, and so was quite unready to meet William and his Dutch fleet, which had a lot of English and Scottish soldiers and exiles on board it. William landed in Devonshire and moved slowly toward London. James had an army, many of whose regiments would have fought faithfully for him

Flight of James, 1688. if he would only have led them; but he turned tail and fled to France; and just before Christmas, 1688, William entered London.

Who is to be King? What was to be done? Was James still King? Had Mary become Queen? Who was to call a Parliament? (Only a King can do this, and it seemed as if there was no King.) William, however, called a "Convention" (which was a Parliament in all but name), and, after some debate, this body decided that James was no longer King, but that William and Mary were

William III and Mary II, 1689. joint King and Queen of England and Ireland. A Scottish Convention declared the same thing for Scotland. A document was drawn up called the "Bill of Rights" which is a sort of second edition of Magna Charta. It fully expresses the idea that the Sovereign of England is a "limited monarch" and that there are a great many things he may not do.

This "Revolution of 1688" was mainly the work of the Whigs, and William has often been called the "Whig Deliverer." Revolutions are bad things, but it is difficult to see how this one could have been avoided. James was a real tyrant, almost as impossible a King for Englishmen as John or "Bloody" Mary I had been; and, since Mary II refused to reign without her husband, and the baby Prince of Wales had fled with his father, the question was perhaps settled in the only satisfactory manner. But England was by no means united by the settlement; William was a foreigner and a foreigner he remained till his death.

CHAPTER X

WILLIAM III TO GEORGE II 1688-1760; THE GROWTH OF EMPIRE

"Brown Bess."

In the days of lace-ruffles, perukes and brocade
    Brown Bess was a partner whom none could
    despise —
An out-spoken, flinty-lipped, brazen-faced jade
    With a habit of looking men straight in the
    eyes —
At Blenheim and Ramillies fops would confess
They were pierced to the heart by the charms
    of Brown Bess.

Though her sight was not long and her weight
    was not small,
    Yet her actions were winning, her language
    was clear;
And every one bowed as she opened the ball
    On the arm of some high-gaitered, grim
    grenadier.
Half Europe admitted the striking success
Of the dances and routs that were given by
    Brown Bess.

.1
8
.1
4

in
Wellington's Time

.1
7
.0

in
Marlborough's Days

When ruffles were turned into stiff leather
    stocks,
  And people wore pigtails instead of perukes,
Brown Bess never altered her iron-gray locks;
    She knew she was valued for more than her
    looks.
"Oh, powder and patches was always my dress,
And I think I am killing enough," said Brown
    Bess.

So she followed her red-coats, whatever they
    did,
  From the heights of Quebec to the plains of
    Assaye,
From Gibraltar to Acre, Cape Town and
    Madrid,
  And nothing about her was changed on the
    way;
(But most of the Empire which now we possess,
Was won through those years by old-fashioned
    Brown Bess).

In stubborn retreat or in stately advance,
  From the Portugal coast to the cork-woods
    of Spain,
She had puzzled some excellent Marshals of
    France
  Till none of them wanted to meet her again:
But later, near Brussels, Napoleon, no less,
Arranged for a Waterloo ball with Brown
    Bess.

She had danced till the dawn of that terrible
    day —
      She danced on till dusk of more terrible
        night,
And before her linked squares his battalions
    gave way
      And her long fierce quadrilles put his lancers
        to flight.
And when his gilt carriage drove off in the press,
"I have danced my last dance for the world!"
    said Brown Bess.

If you go to Museums — there's one in White-
    hall —
      Where old weapons are shown with their
        names writ beneath,
You will find her, upstanding, her back to the
    wall,
      As stiff as a ramrod, the flint in her teeth.
And if ever we English have reason to bless
Any arm save our mothers', that arm is Brown
    Bess!

Reign of William III and Mary II, 1689-94, of William III alone, 1694-1702. THE Bill of Rights had said that "to keep an Army in time of peace was against Law." Only the fact that England was at war for very long periods during the next hundred years saved the Army from being abolished; and at every interval of peace it was reduced far too much for the safety of the country. In 1689 war with France was certain, for, as I told you, William had come to England mainly to in-

duce England to help Holland and other countries whom France was threatening. Also the
French King at once took up the cause of James.

James went to Ireland and called on the
Catholic Irish to help him; French troops and
money were sent after him. Ireland had now
some real wrongs to avenge, for Cromwell's
conquest had been cruel, and many old Irish
families had lost their lands, to make room for
English settlers; these Catholics, therefore,
gave James a good army, with which, early in
1689, he advanced to try and subdue the most
Protestant of the Irish Provinces, Ulster.
But he failed to take the city of Londonderry,
which held out against a most awful siege for
three months and more. It was not till a year
after this that William was able to muster
enough English and Dutch troops to begin
the reconquest of Ireland. He smashed James
to pieces at the Battle of the Boyne, and
drove him once more into exile in 1690; a
year later the war ended with the surrender of
Limerick, which the Catholics had defended
as bravely as the Protestants had defended
Londonderry. Ireland was at last completely
conquered.

William wanted to give, and promised to
give, the defeated Irish Catholics peace and
protection; but the English Parliament in-

James
seeks
Catholic
help in
Ireland

Siege of
London-
derry,
1689.

Battle of
the
Boyne,
1690.

Cruel laws
against
Irish
Catholics,
1692-
1710.

tended that those who provoked the war should pay the expenses of the war. A vast number of estates were therefore again taken from the Catholics and given to the Protestants, and a fresh set of grievances began for Ireland. Harsh laws were also passed in this and the next reign, both in the English and Irish Parliaments, with the intention of stamping out the Catholic religion altogether. They were hardly ever put in force, for the whole Irish people, Catholic and Protestant alike, hated them; and men, after what they had gone through, only wished to live at peace with their neighbours. Harsh laws were also passed and had been passed since 1660 in the English Parliament against Irish trade; for the jealous English merchants feared that Irishmen would make woollen goods, or grow fat bacon, beef, or butter cheaper than England could do. These laws were put in force; and their result in the long run was to make Ireland ripe for rebellion.

The same jealousy was displayed toward Scotland, which was just beginning to have a few small manufactures of its own, and which certainly grew excellent and cheap beef and mutton. Then, too, there was a large party which had clung to King James or was ready to rise for him, especially in the wild Highlands

The laws never enforced. Laws against Irish trade.

Laws against Scottish trade.

north of the Forth and Clyde. The south
and east of Scotland had accepted the Revolution of 1688, and the Presbyterian Church
had again been established. The risings for
King James were put down, though not without tough fighting. But when Scotland asked
to be allowed a share in the trade with our
colonies, the English Parliament answered
with a contemptuous "no"; and the result was
that Scotland growled and growled more and
more throughout the reign of William. But
in the next reign, after long and fierce debates,
the old Scottish Parliament was induced to
vote for union with the English (1708); and
henceforward there was one united Parliament
of Great Britain, and trade was perfectly free
between the two nations. Then began the
great commercial prosperity of Modern Scotland. Within fifty years Glasgow had got an
enormous share of the trade with the British
Colonies and India, and one of the most interesting tales of town history is the story how the
grave merchants of Glasgow got together and
set to work to deepen the river Clyde so as to
make it carry the trade which they knew would
come. The first Glasgow ship for tobacco
sailed to America ten years after the union, and
began what is still one of Glasgow's greatest
industries.

The
Union
with
Scotland,
1708.

The war
with
France,
1689-97.

William III paid far too little attention to these questions of Ireland and Scotland, but his excuse was that he and his Dutch and German allies were engaged in a desperate struggle to save Flanders and the line of the river Rhine from King Louis of France. With great difficulty could he squeeze out of the English Parliament men and money for these wars. None of the English statesmen, Whigs or Tories, really liked the war, and the Tories in particular began to dislike the Revolution which they had helped to make. But wherever the English regiments fought they covered themselves with glory, especially at Steinkirk

Jealousy
against
the army
in Eng-
land.

(1692), and Landen (1693), though they were defeated in both battles. William was a fierce and dogged fighter, but he was not a first-rate general, and France had still the upper hand when a sort of truce was concluded in 1697. Parliament, in which the Tories then had the upper hand, at once reduced the army to 7,000 men.

This was most foolish, as every one knew that old King Louis XIV was only preparing for a fresh war in order to put his own grandson on the throne of Spain, which fell vacant in 1700. The Austrians also claimed the Spanish crown, and it was the plain duty of England to help them. Many Englishmen, however, said, "No, let them fight it out. What does it matter to England? This is what comes of your foreign king," and so on. William, foreigner as he was, knew better. The growing power of France threatened every nation in Europe. The time had gone by when England could afford to stand aside from the quarrels of her neighbours.

William might, however, have failed altogether to convince Englishmen of this if Louis had not made one great mistake. Old King James II died in 1701, and Louis at once recognized his son (the same Prince of Wales who was born in 1688) as "James III." This was the same as dictating to Englishmen who should be their king; and the whole nation voted for war at once. William would have led it to battle as bravely as ever but for his death in 1702. His good wife, Mary, had died childless seven years before, and her sister Anne now became Queen. But Anne, too, was now childless, and so, to find an heir of the old royal blood who was also a Protestant, England would have to go back a long way, in fact to the descendants of James I. James I's daughter Elizabeth had married a German Prince, and that Elizabeth's youngest child, Sophia of Hanover, a very old lady, was the best Protestant heir. She had already a son and a

Death of James II in exile; a new war with France, 1702-13.

Question of the succession again.

grandson, who were one day to be King George I and King George II. No one liked the prospect of a petty German prince as our king, but most people thought anything was better than a Papist, and unfortunately our lawful King, James III, remained a Papist all his days. He could have bought his throne at any moment by turning Protestant, but he was far too honourable to do that.

Parliament becomes all powerful.

Before we leave King William we must notice an important change which took place during his reign, a change which really transferred the *sovereignty* of the country from King to Parliament. To previous kings Parliament had usually voted, at the beginning of the reign,

Taxes.

a certain sum of money to be paid each year out of taxes, which sum, they thought, should be enough to pay all the expenses of governing and defending the country. It never was enough, and extra money had always to be voted for wars. Now, however, William's Parliament voted him only a small sum for his life — enough for himself and his court "to live on"; but the expenses of governing and defending the country, paying the Army and Navy and Civil Service, they only voted from year to year. So since his time the kings have always been obliged to call a Parliament every year whether they wanted to or not — or else to leave Army and Navy without pay.

Further, as William's wars cost a great deal of money, and as Parliament shrank from laying on the heavy taxes which were necessary to pay for them, it allowed the Crown to *borrow* money from any one who would lend it at interest. The interest had to be paid yearly till the loan was repaid. Few such loans ever were repaid, and so a perpetual debt was created called the "National Debt," which has now increased to an enormous amount. But people are always glad to lend money to the Crown, because they know they will get the interest on it paid quite punctually. As long as we pay the interest on this National Debt we are still paying for some of King William's wars and for those of all later sovereigns; but we need not grumble, because, if these great wars had not been fought, there would have been no British Colonies or Empire, and probably no independent Great Britain; our country would have been a province of France. So let King William sleep in peace.

Queen Anne's wars were going to be very successful indeed, though they continued till the last year of her reign. She herself was almost the stupidest woman in her dominions; but she was a good and kindly soul, devoted

Loans and the National Debt.

Anne, 1702-14; her character.

to the Church of England, and had generally
the sense to leave affairs of State to her ministers. She called herself a Tory, and her
ministers called themselves Tories; but they
were going to fight a "Whig War." By this
I mean a war to maintain the Protestant
Kings in England, and to increase the trade
and Empire of England. And so they really
had to act as Whigs. The hero of that war was
John Churchill, Duke of Marlborough, the
greatest soldier England ever produced. He
was not only great in planning a campaign and
in fighting a battle, but also in his care for his
soldiers, their food, their clothing, their comfort and their pay. Also he was very clever
at keeping the allies of Great Britain united.
These allies — Dutch, Austrians, and Germans, were very difficult to manage; for each
thought mainly of their own interests, and
quarrelled with the others continually. But
Marlborough thought of only one thing —
how to beat the French, and very handsomely
did he beat them. At Blenheim (1704), Ramillies (1706), Oudenarde (1708), Malplaquet
(1709), he won victories as complete as those of
Edward III and Henry V. And our redcoats
were foremost in all these battles and won
immortal glory. By 1710 we had swept the
French out of Germany and Flanders, and were

The Duke of Marlborough.

The war of the Spanish Succession, 1702-13.

Battles of Blenheim, etc.

well on the road to Paris. Our Navy had been equally successful; we had beaten a great French fleet off Malaga in Spain, and had taken Gibraltar and the Isle of Minorca. In America our colonists, with little aid from home, had begun to bite away the frontier of the French colony of Canada. All looked like ending in a Treaty of Peace of great glory for Great Britain.

But in Great Britain itself things were not going so well. "Politics" had now become a sort of unpleasant cheating game between a lot of great families of the nobility, Whigs on one side, Tories on the other. Each party strove to control the House of Commons by getting its own friends elected to it, and thus to get itself into office. The Tories, who were also the "High Church" men, hated, or pretended to hate, the war and the Duke of Marlborough. They said, "It is a Whig war, a war for the interests of the merchants, many of them Dissenters too, the brutes! It is a war for foreigners. It is all the fault of those who made that wicked Revolution of 1688 and turned out our natural King. Anne, of course, is a native, but who is to come after her ?— a disgusting, fat German!"

Moreover, the war was expensive, and, whatever ministers may pretend, no one *likes* paying

Tories in power, 1710. The Peace of Utrecht, 1713. taxes.　So these men got the ear of the electors, and a Tory Parliament came in determined to end the war at any price.　The Duke of Marlborough was accused of prolonging it for his own reasons, and being bribed by foreigners to do so.　Of course this was ridiculous nonsense, but he was dismissed from the command, and in 1713 peace with France was concluded at the Treaty of Utrecht, and Great Britain openly deserted her allies.

The British Empire.　Yet so great had been our victories that this treaty of Utrecht could not fail to be of great advantage to us.　It was, in the eyes of all Europe, the foundation of the British Empire. It was like a notice-board: ..

THERE IS A BRITISH EMPIRE:
FOREIGNERS
PLEASE TAKE NOTICE AND KEEP
OFF IT

For we kept not only Gibraltar and Minorca, which were the beginnings of the power of our fleet in the Mediterranean, but also Nova Scotia and Newfoundland, which had been the outworks of French Canada.　Also we secured certain definite rights to trade with the Spanish colonies in South America.　It was on trade the Empire was founded, and by trade it must be maintained.　But, remember, a

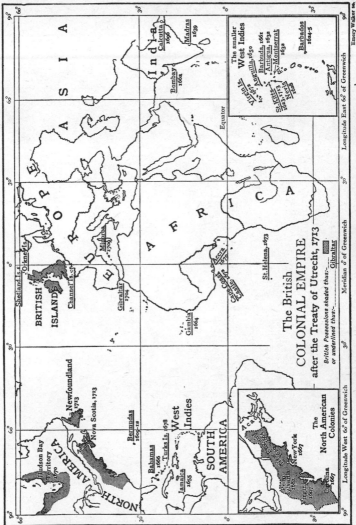

The British
COLONIAL EMPIRE
after the Treaty of Utrecht, 1713

British Possessions shaded thus:......
or underlined thus:...... Gibraltar

Emery Walker sc.

great trade needs a great defence by a great
fleet and a great army. One gets nothing for
nothing in this world.

Yet old King Louis XIV had won his point; France and Spain.
his grandson kept the throne of Spain, to
prevent which we had originally begun to fight.
He did, indeed, give up the "Low Countries"
(which in the Middle Ages we called "Flanders"
and now call Belgium) to our Austrian ally;
and the French and Spanish crowns were not
united on the same head, which was what we
had most feared. But the alliance of France
and Spain remained, with hardly an inter-
ruption, a serious danger for us until 1808; and
we had to fight four great wars against that
alliance if we were to remain an Empire at all.

In Anne's last years, the question again The Suc-cession Question in 1714.
came up — who was to succeed her? The
Tories, who were in power, were *almost* inclined
to say James III, in spite of his being a Papist.
But "almost" is not "quite"; and while the
Tories talked the Whigs were ready to act,
and, on Anne's death in 1714, George I became
King. A Scottish rising on behalf of James A German king; George I, 1714-27.
in 1715 was put down with some difficulty;
and the result was that both English and
Scottish Tories remained sore and disloyal for
many years, always with half an eye to the
"King over the water."

The
Whigs all
powerful.
The Whigs, however, got their King, a dull, honest, heavy fellow, and they allowed him no power whatever. All the officers of State were divided among a few great Whig families. George cared nothing for England, only for his native Hanover. The churchmen growled,

Small in-
fluence of
the Ger-
man
kings.
the country gentlemen growled; but the Dissenters and merchants rejoiced, and made haste to become very rich. Ordinary quiet persons agreed to accept King George, but without enthusiasm. Affection for King and Crown entirely died away until it was revived by the wonderful goodness and high spirit of the great Queen Victoria.

There is practically nothing to record of the reign of George I. The only important law

The "Sep-
tennial
Act,"
1716.
passed was one which said there shall be a new Parliament every seven years, instead of every three years. Abroad there is nothing interesting either. France, which had been very hard hit by the war, only wanted peace. The new King of Spain occasionally growled at our holding Gibraltar, and twice tried to take it from us; which was unlucky for him, as we blew his fleet into the air.

George II,
1727-60;
his cha-
racter.
George I died in 1727, and the first few years of the reign of his son, George II, were almost as quiet as the late reign had been. The new King was a short, ridiculous, red-faced person,

with great goggle-eyes. He cared as little for England and as much for Hanover as his father; but he had fought bravely in Marlborough's wars when he was young, and was always longing to fight somebody. He at least knew how to swear in English, and he was rather too fond of swearing. His prime minister, till 1742, was Sir Robert Walpole, who had ruled his father since 1721. This man, though he shockingly neglected the Army and the Navy, managed money matters remarkably well; and the result was that our trade increased enormously.

Sir Robert Walpole, Prime Minister, 1721-42;

But the price of his neglect of the fighting services had soon to be paid. France, when she had recovered from Marlborough's wars, made a close alliance with Spain, and in 1737 Spain began to attack our trade in America. Sorely against his will, Walpole had to declare war on Spain to defend that trade. France came to Spain's assistance and the war then grew much more serious. It was, in fact, a struggle for power and empire both in America and India and lasted for eight or nine years; and, as our old Austrian and Dutch allies were also attacked by France, she had to send soldiers to Germany and Flanders as well, though she could ill spare them, for it was quite possible that our own island might be invaded. Un-

his neglect of army and navy.

War with Spain, 1739, and France, 1740.

We hire German soldiers. fortunately, we could hire, with our abundant British guineas, Dutch and German troops to fight our battles for us. I cannot imagine a worse plan than this for any country, but it remained a regular British habit down to our grandfathers' days; and it still further increased the unwillingness of our own people to serve in their own army.

Party squabbles. Walpole was dreadfully badgered in Parliament over the badness of this plan, and over many other things, not so much by the few remaining Tory members as by those Whigs who were not actually in office, but wanted to get into office. And when they did come in, they had no better plans to propose. Walpole resigned in 1742, and his successor, Carteret, a far greater man than Walpole, was badgered almost worse, until he too resigned in 1744.

Battles of Dettingen, 1743, and Fontenoy, 1745. Meanwhile King George himself had led British troops to a great victory at Dettingen in Germany, and his second son, the Duke of Cumberland, led them to a defeat almost as glorious at Fontenoy in Flanders, 1745. The French King had been seriously thinking of an invasion of Britain on behalf of the exiled King James III. But the French were justly afraid of

Prince Charles Edward in Scotland. risking their ships against the British navy; and so Prince Charles Edward, son of James III, resolved to strike for himself even without

French help. He landed, with seven followers only, in the Western Highlands of Scotland in the summer of 1745.

He called upon the well-known loyalty of the Highlanders to his family; they answered him as only Highlanders can. Without guns or cavalry, five or six thousand of these men made themselves masters of all Scotland. They could march two miles for every one that the heavily laden English soldiers could march; and of course there were far too few of these regular soldiers in Great Britain. When the Highlanders met them, they would fire one volley from their muskets, throw them down, and charge with the "claymore," the terrible Highland sword. The English soldiers, of whom, indeed, the best regiments were abroad when the Rising began, seemed on this occasion to have forgotten all Marlborough's lessons; their generals were old, slow men; and the rank and file were terrified by the ferocious Highland charges. So Charles was able, in the winter of 1745, with never more than six thousand men, to advance into England as far as Derby. The few great Tory families in England who were supposed to favour the cause of King James III ought now to have come forward and helped his son, but they did nothing. There was, indeed, a real panic in

Rising of the Scottish Highlanders for the exiled Stuart King, 1745.

London; and, if no one rose for King James, very few people seemed anxious to fight for King George. If Charles had gone on then, he might have taken London, but he was persuaded to turn back from Derby, and, in the following spring, was defeated by Cumberland at Culloden in Inverness-shire. That was the end of the Stuart cause in Britain. Cumberland swept the Highlands with fire and sword; and though he failed to catch Prince Charles, who, after five months' wandering, escaped to France, he prevented any further outbreak. Fierce vengeance was taken on the gentlemen who had risen, and there were many cruel executions which might well have been spared.

Battle of Culloden, 1746.

The war with France had been fought in America and India as well as in Germany and Scotland. In the outlaying parts of our Empire, there was hardly any peace between the rival colonists and traders, French and English, even though there might be peace in Europe. You must remember how vast were the spaces, how few the people, in the America of those days; how long, before the time of steamships and telegraphs, it took to get troops or even orders across the Atlantic. In bad weather two months was no uncommon time for a voyage from Bristol to New York; to Calcutta, six or seven months was quite

The war of 1740-8 in America.

usual. The vast but empty French colony French Canada. of Canada had not more than one sixth of the population of the British colonies in North America, then thirteen in number; but it was much better governed, fortified and equipped for war. Our colonists were never united amongst themselves, and did not want to be. They were none too loyal to the mother country, while the French Canadians were thoroughly loyal to France. That is why, between 1740 and 1758, the French were able to press our people in America so hard. Their great object was to occupy the valleys of the great rivers of Ohio and Mississippi. These lay right behind our colonies; and if the French could have held them, the British colonists would have been prevented from expanding westward, which was just what they were doing more and more every year.

In India things were not quite so bad. France The war in India, 1740-8. had an "East India Company" like our own for trading with the native states, and the two companies were natural rivals. Not far from our settlement of Madras lay the French settlement of Pondicherry; opposite to our Calcutta lay the French Chandernagore. Even when there was peace between France and England at home, the rival companies out there used to send their few white soldiers to help some native prince who happened to be at war with another native prince. They also took into their pay native Indians, whom we call Sepoys. They drilled and armed them with European weapons, and made them capital soldiers. An army of two or three hundred French or English soldiers, with perhaps two thousand Sepoys, would beat any native army you liked to name, even if it were fifty thousand strong. In the war of 1740–8 the French did succeed in taking Madras; but, before that war was over, Major Stringer Lawrence and Robert Clive turned the tide of victory again. Clive, who began life as a clerk, was the real founder of the Indian Empire. When peace was made in 1748 by the Treaty of Aix-la-Chapelle, Madras was restored to us.

Robert Clive.

Treaty of Aix-la Chapelle, 1748.

In Europe nothing was settled by that peace; and in India and America there was hardly peace at all. We may cheerfully forget the dull and stupid Whig ministers who ruled England from 1744 to 1756, but in the latter year William Pitt took office. And in 1757 he became an all-powerful war minister. England was then in a very bad way.

William Pitt in office, 1757-61.

The war had just begun again, and the late ministers had so obstinately refused to strengthen the Army or Navy that the King was forced to hire six thousand Germans to defend

Bad state of the country.

the coast of Kent against an expected invasion!
France had taken Minorca from us, and a very
badly fitted-out British fleet, under Admiral
Byng, had failed to rescue it. The fault
was the Minister's, who had neglected the
Navy, but the Nation was angry with the
Admiral, and, to save trouble to the Ministry,
Byng was tried and shot on his own ship.

Pitt changed all this very quickly. He called
upon the Nation outside Parliament, upon
Tory and Whig alike; and while he was War
Minister these evil party names seemed to have
lost their meaning. The spirit of the Nation, now
united as it had never been since the days of
Elizabeth, rose to his call. He terrified the
quarrelsome House of Commons until it voted
him whatever he asked for in the way of men,
money, and ships; he put the militia for home
defence on a new footing; he doubled the
regular army, and enrolled whole regiments of
those very Highlanders who, eleven or twelve
years before, had been fighting against King
George at home. He doubled the number of
our ships of war. As our old ally, Austria,
had gone over to the French, Pitt made a
warm friend of the new German power, the
King of Prussia; and, instead of borrowing
from Germany troops to defend Britain, he
sent regiment after regiment of British troops

Pitt saves
Great
Britain.

Our ally,
Frederick
of
Prussia,
1756-62.

to help Prussia in Germany against France and Austria.

The "Seven Years' War," 1756-63. The war that began in 1756 was called the "Seven Years' War." It was far more clearly a war for empire than any earlier one. "I will win America for us in Germany," was what Pitt said; and what he meant was that France, if thoroughly beaten in Germany, would be unable to spare troops to defend far-away Canada. But, being a thorough man, he also set about winning America in America itself. In America. He even persuaded the disloyal colonists to help us to fight their battles for them, and he paid them to do so. His huge and victorious fleet prevented the French from sending any help to Canada. That colony did, indeed, defend itself down to 1760 with true French gallantry. But when, by an amazing piece of daring, our General Wolfe took Quebec, the Winning of Canada, 1758-60. end was not far off. Three British armies, coming by different roads, gradually closed round the Canadian capital of Montreal, and in 1760 all was over, and North America was British from the Polar ice to Cape Florida; the one little French settlement on the Gulf of Mexico, Louisiana, had lost all importance.

The French driven from India, 1757-60. In India there is a similar story of conquest to be told. There, the native princes had, on the whole, inclined to the French side. One

of them — Surajah Dowlah — took Calcutta
in 1756, and allowed a number of English
prisoners to be suffocated in a horrible dun-
geon called the "Black Hole." Clive, with
about two thousand Sepoys and Englishmen,
came up from Madras to avenge this. He
retook Calcutta, and won a victory, against
odds of twenty-five to one, at Plassy in 1757.
That victory extended the power of the East
India Company far into Bengal. In the region
of Madras our success was equally great; and
in 1761 we took Pondicherry, and swept the
French out of all India. All the native
Princes at once went over to our side.

What was it that gave us, a nation of less
than eight millions of men, these amazing
successes over a nation of at least twenty millions, more naturally warlike, quite as brave,
and much cleverer than ourselves? It was
mainly one thing, *sea power*. The nation that
commands the sea by having the greatest
number of ships and the best-trained sailors
will always beat its rivals in distant lands,
simply because it commands the roads leading
to those lands. If you look back to the beginning of things you will see that it was Cromwell,
it was Elizabeth, nay, it was Henry VIII and
Henry VII, who, by their early and wise care
for our Navy, won for us America and India.

The
secret of
sea
power.

We might, and we usually did, neglect our Navy in time of peace; but in time of war, it had got a mysterious habit of doubling itself, and of discovering great fighting sailors. In this war it had discovered three, Admiral Boscawen, *Battles of Quiberon and Lagos, 1759.* who beat one great French fleet at Lagos, and Admiral Rodney, who played the same game in the West Indies. Perhaps the most daring of all was Sir Edward Hawke, who, as Mr. Newbolt sings, "came swooping from the West" one wild November afternoon onto the French fleet off the rocky coast of Quiberon, and fought a night battle on a lee shore:

Down upon the quicksands, roaring out
    of sight,
Fiercely beat the storm wind, darkly fell
    the night,
But they took the foe for pilot and the
    cannon's glare for light,
When Hawke came swooping from the West!

Death of George II, 1760. Meanwhile old King George II had died in 1760; and his grandson, George III, aged twenty-two, had become King. And now, *George III, 1760-1820.* almost too late, the Spaniards came to the help of their French cousins. Pitt wanted to fly at them and smash them before they had time to declare war on us; but neither the new King nor the other ministers would agree to this; and Pitt, in a fit of anger, resigned his Resignation of Pitt, 1761. office. Yet even when Spain did declare war, Pitt, 1761. at the opening of 1762, the spirit which Pitt War with Spain, 1762. had given to the fighting services carried all before it. We mopped up the remaining French West Indian Islands, and we took from the Spaniards their two richest colonies. Havana in the Isle of Cuba, and Manila in the far Eastern seas.

But when Pitt retired, the union of King, Ministers, Parliament and People, which had George III resolved to put down Whigs. lasted for five out of the seven years of war, was at an end. George III had his very valiant but obstinate mind set on only one thing, to raise the power of the Crown, and to get free from the government of the great Whig families. He meant to take as ministers whom he pleased. He knew that he could not keep such ministers in office if the House of Commons was always against them; and so he set himself to bribe the members of that House. He would distribute offices, pensions, and favours, to its members, until he had made a "Royal" party, which should oppose the "Whig" party. This Royal party would then vote with the ministers whom the King would choose. It took George nearly ten years to do this; but he had a good deal of success in the end. And the nation outside Parliament felt some sympathy

Popularity of George III; his character.

for him; for every one knew how these great Whig families had kept all the richest jobs of the kingdom in their own hands. George was also very popular with the middle classes and the country gentlemen. In fact, he was a sort of Tory; and this new Royal party became a sort of new Tory party. George was at least a thorough Briton, brave, homely, dogged, and virtuous in his private life; but he was in such a hurry to carry out this political job, that he was quite ready to scuttle out of his glorious war, and desert his allies just as Anne's ministers had done in 1713.

Peace of Paris, 1763.

Yet, like the Treaty of Utrecht of 1713, the Treaty of Paris of 1763 could not fail to bring solid advantages to Great Britain. Though we gave back to Spain her rich colonies of Havana and Manila, and took from her only the useless American swamp, called Florida, we recovered Minorca. Though we gave back to France all her great and rich West Indian Islands, we retained several of the smaller ones; though we gave back to her her trading-stations in India, she had to promise never to fortify them again. And, finally, we kept our greatest conquest of all, Canada.

CHAPTER XI

THE AMERICAN REBELLION AND THE GREAT FRENCH WAR 1760-1815; REIGN OF GEORGE III

'Twas not while England's sword unsheathed
    Put half a world to flight,
Nor while their new-built cities breathed
    Secure behind her might;
Not while she poured from Pole to Line
    Treasure and ships and men —
These worshippers at Freedom's shrine
    They did not quit her then!

Not till their foes were driven forth
    By England o'er the main —
Not till the Frenchman from the North
    Had gone, with shattered Spain;
Not till the clean-swept ocean showed
    No hostile flag unrolled,
Did they remember what they owed
    To Freedom — and were bold!

Soon after the peace of 1763, we began to perceive one result of the conquest of Canada

The Rebellion of the American Colonies, 1776.

which few people had expected. Our American colonies, having no French to fear any longer, wanted to be free from our control altogether. They utterly refused to pay a penny of the two hundred million pounds that the war had cost us; and they equally refused to maintain a garrison of British soldiers. They intended to shake off all our restrictions on their trade, and to buy and sell in whatever market they could find. When our Parliament proposed in 1764 to make them pay a small fraction of the cost of the late war, they called it "oppression," and prepared to rebel. "We are Whigs," they said: "Whigs always resist oppression. You English Whigs did so in 1688."

What the English Whigs thought of it.

There were two results from this: In the first place, the great Whig families were already sore at King George's attempts to take his ministers without consulting them. And, when they saw the King and his ministers set upon compelling the Americans to pay the tax, they began to denounce the very things of which they had formerly been the champions, namely, the Empire, the Army, and the Navy. America was right, they said, to resist such "oppression." Even the great William Pitt, now Earl of Chatham, said this. And so the whole meanings of the words "Whig" and "Tory" were completely changed. The Whig became a person who cared little for the Empire, and, occasionally, even supported the enemies of his country, just as the Tory of Anne's reign had done. And the Tories became, for a season, the true patriots, as the Whigs of Anne's reign had been.

The second result was that we had to fight our colonies, and that we failed to beat them. It was a hopeless business from the first. The distance was too great, the spaces of America were too vast for us to hold by force, even if we had won in battle. The quarrels in our Parliament were too fierce to allow of success. We had no great minister at home, and no great general in America. The colonists called a Congress at Philadelphia; declared themselves to be independent; and in 1776 took the name of the "United States of America." Blood had already been shed when this happened. A real hero, patient, resourceful, and brave, called George Washington, commanded the American army. We never sent enough troops; we had not, in fact, enough troops to send. Though we often won battles, we suffered some very severe disasters.

The Americans very soon sought French help, and France was delighted at such a chance of avenging her losses in the former war. The French fleet, though small, had been much

War with America, 1775-82.

The "United States of America," 1776.

They ask French help, 1778.

improved since that war, and was able to draw away our ships from the coast of America to all quarters of the world. We were just able to defend the rest of our Empire (except Minorca, which we now lost again); but not to beat our colonists at the same time. Spain, and even our ally Holland, soon joined France; and for a few months, we had the navies of all the world against us. So, when Lord Cornwallis, with seven thousand men, was obliged to surrender to a French and American force at Yorktown in 1781, we determined to withdraw from America; after which, having our hands free, we finished the naval war victoriously in other quarters of the world. Rodney smashed a great French fleet in the West Indies; and Lord Heathfield, at Gibraltar, beat off the siege of that rock, which had lasted for three years. By a treaty signed in 1783 we acknowledged the Independence of America, gave back Florida and Minorca to Spain, and some small West Indian Islands, as well as Senegal in West Africa, to France. These were serious losses; yet France had been even harder hit by the war than we had been. She had hoped, in return for her help to receive valuable trading privileges with America; but the Americans showed no more gratitude to her than they had previously shown to us, and she received none.

Naval war with France, 1778-83.

Peace of Versailles, 1783.

The snow lies thick on Valley Forge
  The ice on the Delaware,
But the poor dead soldiers of King George
  They neither know nor care ——

Not though the earliest primrose break
  On the sunny side of the lane,
And scuffling rookeries awake
  Their England's spring again.

They will not stir when the drifts are gone
  Or the ice melts out of the bay,
And the men that served with Washington
  Lie all as still as they.

They will not stir though the mayflower blows
  In the moist dark woods of pine,
And every rock-strewn pasture shows
  Mullein and columbine.

Each for his land, in a fair fight,
  Encountered, strove, and died,
And the kindly earth that knows no spite
  Covers them side by side.

She is too busy to think of war;
  She has all the world to make gay,
And, behold, the yearly flowers are
  Where they were in our fathers' day!

Golden-rod by the pasture wall
  When the columbine is dead,
And sumach leaves that turn, in fall,
  Red as the blood they shed.

Factions
in British
Parlia-
ment,
1764-83.

All this time there were fierce quarrels in
Parliament, between Whigs and Tories, on
many questions besides the war. Every act
of Government, good or bad, was torn to pieces
and called "infamous" by the Whigs, some of
whom sought for popularity by writing in the
newspapers, and even by appealing to the
passions of the London mob. That mob more
than once broke loose and enjoyed some highly
exciting riots, in suppressing which King George
showed great personal courage. One of the
cries raised at this time, both in and outside
Parliament, was for a better representation
of the people of Britain in the House of Commons. It was really a very reasonable cry,
for the existing system was absurd.

Cry for
Reform
of House
of Com-
mons.

By that system each county sent two members to Parliament, whatever its population.
And in the counties only actual *owners* of land
could vote at elections. You might be enormously rich and have a long lease of an enormous
estate; but unless you owned land you had no
vote. Then the boroughs, which also sent two
members each, were still the same towns which

The
"Rotten
Bor-
oughs."

had sent members to the Tudor Parliaments.
From many of these towns, all trade, riches and
importance had long departed, and some boroughs had hardly any inhabitants at all!
Side by side with these were great cities grown
and growing up, which sent no members to Parliament. Now, if the Tories had been wise,
they would have taken up this question, and
made a proper and moderate "reform" of the
House of Commons. The Whigs, who called
themselves "champions of the people," could
hardly with decency have opposed it. But
when William Pitt, the younger son of the William
great Minister of the Seven Years' War, took younger.
up the question in 1785, he could get very little
support from his own party. So this question
fell into the hands of noisy agitators outside
Parliament, who cried out for a "Radical
Reform," and got the name of "Radicals."

The ten years that followed the peace of His first
1783 were years of great prosperity in Britain. 1784-
The Americans continued to trade with us as 1801.
before, though, of course, we could no longer
compel them to do so. Our Indian Empire Our
had been enormously increased since 1761 by Empire.
Clive and Warren Hastings, and by a long
line of heroic soldiers and statesmen. The
East India Company was now a sovereign
power, and the greatest military power in India.

Parliament had begun to take notice of it, not always favourable or wise notice, and passed laws to help it to govern its territories. The Crown now appointed a Governor-General, a council, and judges for British India. One of the favourite tricks of the Whigs was to accuse the Company and its agents of cruelty, extortion, and so on. The first Governor-General, Warren Hastings, was so accused, and though he was acqu tted, his trial dragged on for many years. Still further away the voyages of Captain Cook had recently revealed to Europe the huge continent of Australia, the islands of New Zealand, and numerous other islands in the Pacific Ocean. Our first colonies began to be planted in Australia in 1787.

Discovery of Australia, 1774-6.

The Industrial Revolution.

At home great changes were beginning which were going to turn Britain from a corn-growing and wool-growing country into the workshop of the wo d. These changes have got the name of the "Industrial Revolution." They took more than a century to work out, and the result of them has been that we now buy nearly all our food from distant lands, and buy it with the goods which we make in our great cities, principally iron, cotton, and woollen goods. It is sometimes a little difficult to arrange for an uninterrupted supply of food for forty million people. Until about the middle

of the eighteenth century the south and east
of England had been the richest counties.   Now   Iron and
the north and west, South Wales and Southern   coal.
Scotland quickly began to supplant them
because in these parts iron and coal are found
close together.   The invention of numerous
machines also began to save hand-labour,
and weaving and spinning, which were formerly
done in country cottages, were now done in
great factories, which could only exist in great
towns.   The most important of all discoveries
of this period is that of the steam engine.
For, by the force of steam, all machines could   Steam
be worked for all manufactures much more   engines.
cheaply and powerfully than by hand-labour
or by water-mills.   England used steam in all
her manufactures twenty years before any
other nation, and so no other nations could at
first compete with her.   The sad result has   Increase
been that the country districts have gradually   of towns.
been deserted and the towns have become more
important than the farming land.   But the
full result was not generally realized until
far into the nineteenth century.   At first,   Lack of
the faster population increased in the towns,   food.
the greater was the demand for corn to feed
it.   Very little corn could yet be brought from
abroad, because few countries had any corn
to spare before the vast spaces of America and

Canada were cultivated. So the price of corn began to go up and up; and, though wages went up too, they never went up fast enough.

The poor rate. When the harvest fell short, the poor were often very badly off for food, and had to have relief given them out of the Poor Rates. Poor Rates had existed since the reign of Elizabeth, but had not increased much or been felt as a great burden until this period; now they began to increase enormously. There were also riots in every year of bad harvest, and many of these

Riots. riots were directed against the new machinery, which foolish men said "took the bread out of their mouths." In that belief the rioters made a point of breaking the machines. So, side by side with the enormous increase of the country's wealth, there was often found increase of misery and discontent among the poor. Foolishly, but naturally, the poor used to blame the government and the laws for their misery. But the condition of the lowest class of the people, both in the old and the new towns, had long been attracting the attention of serious people. In the reigns of George I and George II, though many bishops and clergy did their duty earnestly, there were many who did not, and perhaps we may admit that the Church of England had, as a whole, rather "gone to sleep." It was this which gave such effect to the preaching of the brothers John and Charles Wesley from about 1730. They went into the poorest slums and the most deserted parishes and preached, often in the open air, the need of repentance and the duty of listening to that message. The result was the foundation of the "Methodist" and Wesleyan Communities, which gradually grew into dissenting churches, separated, much against the original intentions of their founder, from the National Church. John Wesley lived to a great age and continued to preach till the day of his death in 1791.

The Wesleyan movement, 1730-91.

It was during the long ministry of William Pitt the younger, the son of the man who won Canada for us, that these great changes began to bear their first fruit. Pitt was Prime Minister from 1783 to 1801, and again from 1804 to 1806. For nine years he kept the peace, and undertook an infinite number of valuable reforms in every department of the State save one. He simplified taxes and the Customs' duties and the method of collecting them; he began to pay off the National Debt. He tried to reform the House of Commons, to abolish the cruel trade of carrying slaves from Africa to the West Indies; he tried to pacify Ireland and give it perfect free trade with Britain; and he would have liked to abolish

Pitt's wisdom and reforms, 1784-93.

the laws which still shut out the Catholics from Parliament. Every wise and moderate change which took place during the nineteenth century had already been conceived by this great and wise man. But many of his proposals were upset or spoiled either by the opposition of the Whigs, the stupidity of the Tories, or the prejudices of King George. The one mistake Pitt made was in refusing to set the Army and Navy on a proper footing to meet a future war. He seemed to think that Europe was going to be at peace forever; whereas the greatest war that had ever threatened Great Britain was just going to burst upon her and continue for twenty-two years. Then all Pitt's projects for reform had to be thrown to the winds and the nation had to harden itself to fight to the death.

His neglect of the Army and Navy.

This great war was caused by the "French Revolution." It was the old story of France desiring to dominate the world; and it began in this way: The French people had a series of real grievances against their clumsy, stupid, old-fashioned system of government by an "absolute" king; and they demanded a parliamentary system and a "limited" monarchy like our own. But at the first touch the whole fabric of old France fell to pieces. Kings, nobles, society itself were hurled down; all in the name

The French Revolution, 1789.

of some imaginary "natural rights" of every-
body to have an equal share in government.
A Republic was set up; King Louis XVI was
put to death. A new kind of "Gospel" was
preached; "all men are equal," "all government
is tyranny, all religion is a sham," "down
with everything and up with ourselves" ("ourselves" being the bloodthirsty mobs of Paris
and other great cities). This precious Republic proceeded to offer its alliance to all the
peoples of Europe who wished to abolish their
kings, and "recover their liberty." It declared
war on Austria and Prussia, and began by invading Belgium and threatening Holland, which
had been our ally since 1688.

France
eager for
war,
1792.

Then, at the opening of 1793, Pitt felt bound
to interfere. The nation was heartily at his
back. Scenes of the utmost horror and cruelty
had taken place in France, and the French people, once the most civilized in Europe, seemed to
have gone mad. There were a few noisy politicians in Britain, both in and outside Parliament, who sympathized with the French, and
cried out for "Radical Reform" and a "National Convention" of the whole British people;
but they were very few. The worst of them
was the Whig orator, Charles Fox, who had
rejoiced over every disaster of his country
during the war against America. A good deal

England
must
fight,
1793.

Noisy
Whig
politi-
cians.

of wild nonsense was also written in some of
the Whig newspapers. Daily newspapers began
early in the eighteenth century; but they were
still expensive, and, as yet, few of the poorer
classes could read, so the newspapers used to
be passed from hand to hand, or read aloud
in the public-house. On the whole, the voice
of the newspapers was thoroughly patriotic.

Ireland.
1782-
1800. But if there were few sympathizers with
France in Britain, there were many in Ireland.
Ireland still had real grievances, though during
the last thirty years they had steadily been
removed. She had shown little gratitude for
their removal, and many Irishmen had openly
sympathized with the American rebellion. In
1782 her Parliament had been declared to be
absolutely free from the laws of the British
Parliament, and there was therefore a real
danger that Ireland might refuse to go to war
Catholics
and Pro-
testants
in Ireland. to help Great Britain. The Catholics were
still shut out from this Parliament; but, ex-
cepting in Ulster, nearly all the poorer Irishmen were Catholics. Pitt, as I told you,
wanted to admit Catholics to both Parliaments;
but it was not the time to make such a great
change, when Britain was in the middle of a
dangerous war, and when the mass of the Irish
peasants, poor, disloyal, and ignorant, were
quite ready to welcome a French invasion of

Ireland. From 1795 there was almost a state of civil war between Irish Protestants and Catholics; and, in 1798, the latter openly rebelled. England had very few troops to spare, and the rebellion took nearly a year to put down. French invasion was hourly expected, though only once a very few French troops were able to land. When the rebellion was over, Pitt rightly decided that the best thing for both countries was to abolish the Irish Parliament, and to make one united Parliament for the two islands (1800). In this united Parliament Pitt intended to allow the Catholics to sit; but King George foolishly and obstinately refused to agree, and so Pitt had to resign the office of Prime Minister, which he had held for eighteen years.

And now for the "great war." For Britain it would necessarily be a sea war, and therefore a war for empire, trade, and colonies. For France, as far as she could make it so, it would be a land war, since it was Europe that France wanted to conquer, not sea or colonies. At first, as I told you, she professed to be conquering other states for their own good, "to liberate them from their tyrants," and all that sort of nonsense. But most nations, even those that really were badly governed, soon found out that French invasion was much

Civil War and Rebellion in Ireland, 1798.

The Union of the Parliaments, 1800.

Resignation of Pitt, 1801.

The war abroad.

France intends to conquer Europe.

worse than any amount of bad government by their own "tyrants." So nation after nation rose and fought against France, either one by one or in great alliances of nations. All were beaten; France was the greatest land power in the world, and her soldiers the bravest, cleverest, and fiercest fighters. All the nations in the world appealed to England to help them with the one thing which all knew she had got in heaps, money. We actually paid Dutchmen, Prussians, Austrians, Spaniards, Russians and even Turks to fight for their own interests against France.

English commerce, 1793-1815

How could we afford to do this? Simply because of the power of our Navy, which in a few years became so great, that it was able to crush the commerce and to take the colonies of any nation that would not fight against France. Soon it was only in Britain that people could buy the goods of the far East and the far West, silk, coffee, tobacco, sugar, tea, spice. And at last only in Britain could they buy manufactured articles at all. Even the very Frenchmen who fought us had to buy the clothes and shoes they wore from English merchants!

The Naval War, 1793-7.

This control of the world's trade did not come to us at once, and not without hard fighting. Pitt, as I told you, had neglected the Army and Navy. Our admirals were old, our generals were at first very stupid. We sent some troops to help the Dutch, and they were very badly beaten. Holland became a daughter-republic of France, and Belgium became a French province. The poor Dutch did not gain much by the exchange, for the British navy simply took away all their colonies notably Ceylon and the Cape of Good Hope, just as it was taking the French West Indian Islands. Nearer home our fleet did not do so well. The French Republic did not have so good a navy as the old French Monarchy had had; but its sailors made up in gallantry what they lacked in skill and efficiency, and it was not until 1797 that we won a great naval battle in European waters. The Spaniards had been forced into the French alliance, and in that year Sir John Jervis and Captain Nelson (soon to be Lord Nelson) utterly defeated a big French and Spanish fleet at Cape St. Vincent on the Spanish coast. *Battle of Cape St. Vincent, 1797.*

It was just at this time that the greatest soldier that ever lived came to lead the French — Napoleon Bonaparte. He appeared first as a victorious general in 1796, then as "First Consul" (that is, President) of the French Republic, 1799; then in 1804 as "Emperor of the French." By this time France had *Napoleon Bonaparte becomes Emperor of the French, 1804.*

given up all idea of delivering peoples from "tyrants," and simply meant to conquer all the world for her own benefit. Napoleon at once saw that this was impossible as long as Britain remained free and victorious at sea.

He means to invade England.

To invade Britain, or to destroy in some other way the wealth and commerce of Britain, became his one desire. But to invade Britain while our fleet watched outside all French harbours, while it prevented French ships from sailing out, and smashed them if they did, was not so easy. The mere fear of invasion was enough to set the hearts of all Britons beating.

The Volunteers, 1803-5.

Volunteers flocked to arms from every parish in our island; and by 1804 we had nearly half a million men in fighting trim in a population of little over eleven millions. If we were to keep the same proportion to-day, we ought to have nearly three millions of men under arms. How many have we got?

Battles of the Nile, 1798, and Copenhagen, 1800.

But in truth Napoleon's chances of invading us were not great. Nelson had broken his Mediterranean fleet to splinters at the Battle of the Nile, 1798, and had also finished a Danish fleet (which had been got ready to help France) at the Battle of Copenhagen in 1800. A few

Peace of Amiens, 1802-3.

months of peace, 1802-3, followed the retirement of Pitt from the Government. But the war began again in 1803; Pitt came back in

the next year, and governed Britain until his War again, 1803-15.
death at the beginning of 1806. The years
1803–4–5 were the most dangerous. Napoleon
had got a great army at Boulogne (which is
almost within sight of the shore of Kent, not
three hours' sail, with a fair wind, from Folkestone), ready to be rowed across the Channel
in large, flat-bottomed boats.

But what was the use of that without a French The critical year, 1805.
fleet to protect the flat-bottoms? If they had
tried to get across unprotected, a single British
warship could have pounded them into a red
rice-pudding in a few minutes; and so our real
task was to watch the French harbours and
prevent their ships of war getting out. The
final struggle came in 1805. The French
Admiral Villeneuve managed to get out from
Toulon; drove off the British force which was
watching the Spanish ports, and so freed the
Spanish fleet. He then sailed across the Atlan- Battle of Trafal-gar, Oct. 18, 1805.
tic and back again, in the hope of drawing all
British ships away from the Channel. After
a long chase Lord Nelson met him off the
Spanish coast, and won the Battle of Trafalgar
in October, 1805. It was almost a dead calm
all the morning as the great fleets crept slowly
toward each other — they must have looked
like moving thunder-clouds. Lord Nelson's
famous signal "England expects that every

man will do his duty " was spelled out in little
flags from the mast of his great ship the *Victory*.
And every man did.   Almost the whole French
and Spanish fleets were there sunk or taken prisoners.   No such victory had been won at sea
since the Greeks beat the Persians at Salamis
nearly five hundred years before Christ.   Nelson
was killed in the battle; but the plan of invasion
was over and Napoleon never resumed it.   The
French navy hardly recovered from this defeat
before our own days.   You can see the *Victory*
still moored in Portsmouth harbour, and can
go into the little dark cabin in which Nelson
died, happy in spite of mortal pain, because
he just lived long enough to hear of England's
triumph.

French
victories
on the
Continent,
1805-9.

The remaining colonies of France and her
allies were gradually conquered during the
next ten years.   But at first this seemed to
help little toward freeing the continent of Europe
which, by 1807, France had subdued right up
to the Russian frontier.   Prussia had been
beaten to pieces in 1806; Austria which, on the
whole, had been the most steady of Napoleon's enemies, was beaten for the third time
in 1809, and was half inclined to make an
alliance with him; but by that time Napoleon
had run his head against something which was
going to destroy him.

NELSON·SHOT·AT·THE·BATTLE·OF·TRAFALGAR·
·OCTOBER·21·1805·

Much the worst governed, most ignorant, most backward nation in Europe, was Spain. Napoleon thought it would be easy to put one of his brothers on the throne of Spain, and one of his generals on the throne of Portugal. Spain was, besides, the oldest ally of France; but when Napoleon tried this plan in 1808, she became at once his fiercest enemy. She did not want to be "reformed" or better governed; she wanted to keep her stupid, cruel Catholic kings and priests. Both Spain and Portugal at once cried out for British help; and, as the road by sea was in our hands, we began at once to send help in money, and very soon in men. With the men we sent *a man*. "In war," said Napoleon himself, "it is not so much men as a man that counts." Sir Arthur Wellesley, one day to be known as the Duke of Wellington, was perhaps not so great a soldier as Marlborough or as Napoleon. His previous experience of war had been mostly in India, where, under his brother, the Marquis Wellesley, who was Governor-General of India, he had won, in 1803 and 1804, great victories over enormous swarms of native cavalry called Mahrattas. But he was the most patient and skilful leader we had had since Marlborough, and he had complete confidence in himself and in his power to beat the French.

Napoleon attacks Spain, 1808.

British troops sent to Portugal. 1808.

Sir Arthur Wellesley.

The Peninsular War; Battle of Vimeiro, 1808.

He landed in Portugal in 1808, won a great battle at Vimeiro, and early in the next year had driven the French back into Spain. He then made Lisbon (the capital city of Portugal) his "base of operations." The British fleet was able continually to bring supplies, money, food and men to Lisbon. Wellington fortified the approach to the city very strongly, and was able to repel an enormous French army which came to attack him there in 1810. He followed it up into Spain as it retreated; and year by year advanced further into Spain, winning battle after battle. But each winter he fell back upon his base. The fierce patriotism of the Spanish peasants, who killed every Frenchman they met, helped us enormously, though in the battles their armies were of little use to us, and their generals worse than useless. At last in 1813 came a year in which Wellington did not need to retreat into Portugal. He won the great Battle of Vittoria in June, and then drove the French back in headlong flight over the Pyrenees. Early in 1814 our men were fighting their way into that French province, which, five hundred years before, we used to call "English Aquitaine."

Welling-ton's advance, 1810-11-12.

Battle of Vittoria, 1813.

Napoleon attacks Russia, 1812; his defeat.

And meanwhile in 1812, at the other end of Europe, Napoleon himself had suffered an even worse disaster. He had invaded Russia, a country whose people were as ignorant, as backward and as patriotic as the Spaniards. The greatest French army that was ever put on foot had starved and been frozen among the snows of Russia. As its broken remnants retreated through Germany, the Prussians, whom the French had cruelly ill-treated since 1806, jumped upon them, and called on all other Germans to do the same. The Austrians joined in. England poured money into the hands of all who would fight the French. Since Pitt's death, until 1812 there had only been one great British Minister, George Canning; but he had resigned his office in 1809. Now in 1812 Lord Castelreagh, a minister almost as great as Pitt, came to the front, and it was his government that really finished the war. Napoleon could, indeed, collect a new army in 1813, but it was never so good as the one he had lost in Russia; and it suffered a fearful defeat at Leipzig. After a most gallant defence of the French roads which lead to Paris, Napoleon was compelled by his own generals to resign the throne, and Louis XVIII, the heir of the old French monarchy, was recalled to France as king in 1814. Napoleon was allowed to retire to the little Italian island of Elba, but he did not stay there long.

In order to arrange a general peace, the

Europe awake to resist France, 1813-14.

Lord Castlereagh, 1812-15.

Napoleon abdicates, 1814.

great powers of Europe sent ambassadors to

Congress
of Vienna,
1815;
return of
Napoleon,
March,
1815.
Vienna. But while they were doing this, in March, 1815, Napoleon escaped from Elba, landed in France, and called on the French people to follow him once more. Nearly all Frenchmen were tired of war; but, like other

War of
1815.
brave fellows, they loved glory, and Napoleon's name spelt glory for them. They forgot his tyranny and his folly, and they proclaimed him Emperor yet again. Europe was utterly taken by surprise, and nearly all its armies had been dismissed. But the Prussians and English were more ready for fighting than the Russians and Austrians, and so within three months they were able to collect over two hundred thousand men for the defence of Belgium. Napoleon's new army was nearly three hundred thousand strong; but he only took about half of it to attack Belgium early in the summer of 1815.

The Duke of Wellington and the Prussian

Battles of
Quatre
Bras and
Ligny,
June 16,
1815.
general, Marshal Blucher, were waiting for him in a long line to the south of Brussels. On June 16th, Napoleon's left wing fought a fearful drawn battle with Wellington at Quatre Bras, and his right wing just managed to beat Blucher at Ligny. On the 17th there was no fighting; but the Prussians had fallen back eastward, and had lost touch with the English.

So, on the 18th, Wellington and the English army, ninety thousand strong, had to bear, for seven hours, the attacks of a hundred and twenty thousand Frenchmen at Waterloo. Wellington knew that Blucher would come and help him as fast as he could; but the roads were heavy from rain, and Blucher had been fearfully hard-hit two days before. But at last he came, though his men did not get into action till about 4.30 P. M., and did not produce much effect on the French for two hours more. We had then been defending our position since 11 A. M. But soon after seven we began to advance, and the night closed with a headlong flight of the French Emperor and his army on the road to Paris. Battle of Waterloo, June 18, 1815.

This battle of Waterloo ended the Great War; the last war, let us hope, that we shall ever have to fight against the French, who are now our best friends. Long ago Pitt had said "England has saved herself by her exertions, she will save Europe by her example." In 1815 she had indeed done both. Peace at last, 1815.

When the final treaty was made in that year, our gains in actual territory were small. We gave back the greater part of the colonies we had taken from France and her allies, keeping only the West Indian island of Tobago, the Island of Mauritius in the Indian Ocean, The gains of Great Britain at the Peace.

the Dutch colonies of Ceylon and the Cape of
Good Hope, and the little Dutch province
of Guiana in South America. In the Mediterranean, we kept the island of Malta, but gave
back Minorca to Spain. Our real reward,
then, came in the commerce of the world,
which during the war had passed wholly into
our hands.

THE FRENCH WARS.

The boats of Newhaven and Folkestone and
    Dover,
To Dieppe and Boulogne and to Calais cross
    over;
And in each of those runs there is not a square
    yard
Where the English and French haven't fought
    and fought hard!

If the ships that were sunk could be floated
    once more,
They'd stretch like a raft from the shore to
    the shore,
And we'd see, as we crossed, every pattern and
    plan
Of ship that was built since sea-fighting began.

There'd be biremes and brigantines, cutters
    and sloops,
Cogs, carracks and galleons with gay gilded
    poops —
Hoys, caravels, ketches, corvettes and the rest,
As thick as regattas, from Ramsgate to Brest.

But the galleys of Cæsar, the squadrons of
    Sluys,
And Nelson's crack frigates are hid from our eyes,
Where the high Seventy-fours of Napoleon's
    days,
Lie down with Deal luggers and French *chasse-*
    marées.

They'll answer no signal — they rest on the
    ooze
With their honey-combed guns and their skele-
    ton crews —
And racing above them, through sunshine or
    gale,
The Cross-Channel packets come in with the
    Mail.

Then the poor sea-sick passengers, English and
    French,
Must open their trunks on the Custom-house
    bench,
While the officers rummage for smuggled cigars
And nobody thinks of our blood-thirsty wars!

CHAPTER XII

GEORGE III TO GEORGE V, 1815–1911

The last
ninety-
five years. THE period of English History which remains
for me to tell you about will bring us down to
our own days. It is a much more difficult story
to understand than any that I have already told
you. It is also much more difficult to write
about.

For people hold such diverse opinons about
the events of the present day and of the last
hundred years. These opinions are very often
the result of their upbringing; "we have heard
with our ears and our fathers have told us."
Men are still alive who were born before Waterloo was fought. As you get older you will
form opinions about these events for your-
selves; and so it is desirable for me, in this last
chapter, rather to state what did take place
than to try to guide your opinions. And it
will be easier to do this if you, my readers, will
allow me to treat the period as all one, rather
than narrate the events year by year.

On the whole, the progress of Great Britain

during the past ninety-five years has been toward what is called "Democracy," a long word meaning "Government by the people." This form of government may be said to be still "on its trial." Let us hope that it will prove a great success. It will only do so if all classes of the people realize that they have duties as well as rights, and if each class realizes that every other class has rights as well as itself.

Progress toward Democracy.

Five sovereigns have reigned and died during these ninety-five years, and the sixth is now upon the throne. George III had long been blind and insane when he died in 1820, and it was the eldest of his seven sons who became King in that year as George IV. This man had been acting as Prince Regent for his insane father since 1810. He was naturally clever and had some kind of selfish good nature, but he was mean, cowardly, and an incredible liar. Some famous lies he told so often that at last he got to believe them himself; for instance, he was fond of saying that he had been present at the Battle of Waterloo, whereas he had never seen a shot fired in his life.

Five sovereigns in these ninety-five years George IV, 1820-30.

He was succeeded in 1830 by a stupid honest old gentleman, his brother, William IV, who, as a young man, had been nicknamed "Silly Billy." There was no harm in King William, but there was little active good, and so the

William IV, 1830-37.

influence of the Crown, both upon private and public life, was very slight when he died in 1837. His heir was his niece Victoria, a girl of eighteen of whom little was then known, but of whose goodness and high spirit, stories were already being told.

Victoria the Great, 1837-1901,

"Who will be King, Mamma," she said, when she was twelve years old, "when Uncle William dies?" "You will be Queen, my dear." "Then I must be a very good little girl now," she replied. In this wonderful lady the spirit of all her greatest ancestors seemed to have revived, the burning English patriotism of the Tudors, the Scottish heart of the Stuarts, the courage of Edward III, the wisdom of Edward I, Henry II and Alfred. And all were softened and beautified by womanly love and tenderness. No sovereign ever so unweariedly set herself to win the love of her people, to be the servant of her people. And her people rewarded her with a love that she had more than deserved. Her reign of sixty-three years will always be remembered in history by her name; it was the "Victorian Age." Her husband was her own cousin, the wise and good Prince Albert of Saxe-Coburg-Gotha, a small State in central Germany. She was succeeded by her eldest son, Edward VII, whose too short reign closed only after this book was

her character.

Edward VII, 1901-1910.

begun.   All the Empire is still in mourning
for him, the wise and prudent statesman, the
peace-lover, the peacemaker of Europe, the
noble English gentleman.

The result of the reigns of Victoria and George V, 1910
Edward VII has been to lift the Crown again
to a position which it had not occupied in
men's minds since the death of Elizabeth.
It is not with our lips only that we are loyal
to King George V, it is with our hearts also.
The crown is not only the "golden circle" that
binds the Empire together; it is the greatest
thing in that Empire.

THE BELLS AND THE QUEEN, 1911.

"Gay go up and gay go down
To ring the Bells of London Town."
When London Town's asleep in bed
You'll hear the Bells ring overhead,
        In excelsis gloria!
        Ringing for Victoria,
Ringing for their mighty mistress — ten years
        dead!

Here's more gain than Gloriana guessed,
    Than Gloriana guessed or Indies bring —
Than golden Indies bring.   A Queen confessed,
    A Queen confessed that crowned her people
        King.

Her people King, and crowned all Kings above,
  Above all Kings have crowned their Queen
      their love —
Have crowned their love their Queen, their
    Queen their love!

Denying her, we do ourselves deny,
  Disowning her are we ourselves disowned.
Mirror was she of our fidelity,
  And handmaid of our destiny enthroned;
The very marrow of Youth's dream, and still
Yoke-mate of wisest Age that worked her will!

Our fathers had declared to us her praise.
  Her praise the years had proven past all
      speech.
And past all speech our loyal hearts always,
  Always our hearts lay open, each to each;
Therefore men gave their treasure and their
    blood
To this one woman — for she understood!

Four o' the clock!   Now all the world is still.
O London Bells to all the world declare
The Secret of the Empire — read who will!
The Glory of the People — touch who dare!

THE BELLS:
    Power that has reached itself all kingly
        powers,
        St. Margaret's: By love o'erpowered —
        St. Martin's: By love o'erpowered —
        St. Clement Danes': By love o'erpowered,
            The greater power confers!

THE BELLS:
> For we were hers, as she as she was ours,
> *Bow Bells:* And she was ours —
> *St. Paul's:* And she was ours —
> *Westminster:* And she was ours,
> As we, even we, were hers!

THE BELLS:
> As we were hers!

The next greatest thing, probably every one will admit, is the Parliament of the United Kingdom. During these ninety-five years that Parliament has undergone considerable changes. The House of Lords has been very much increased in numbers, but has not been altogether strengthened by this increase. It still represents, as it has always represented, the wealthy people of the kingdom. When the only wealth was in land, the House of Lords consisted almost wholly of great landowners. Now that the traders have more wealth than the landowners, rich manufacturers and other great employers of labour have been made peers, though they also have nearly always bought land to support their dignity.

The House of Commons has undergone a still greater change. I told you in the last chapter what serious need there was in the eighteenth century for a "Reform" of that

The British Parliament, 1815-1910

The House of Lords.

The House of Commons.

house, and how, during the twenty-two years of
the Great War, that and all other reforms had
to be put off. A very small knot of Whigs
had never ceased to urge that reform even
during the war. The foremost of these was
Charles, Earl Grey.

Mistakes
of the
Tories,
1815-32.

I have had to scold the Whigs a good deal
during the reign of George III, and I am afraid
I shall now have to scold the Tories for their
attitude during the first fifteen of these ninety-
five years. They held power right up to 1830,
and it was obviously their duty to take up this
and many other questions in a serious and
"modern" spirit. They consisted of two sec-
tions, the enlightened Tories, like Mr. Canning
and Sir Robert Peel, who had sat at the feet
of William Pitt; and the stick-in-the-mud
Tories, like Lord Sidmouth and Lord Eldon,
who were opposed to any change in any department of life. I think it was strange that the
former as well as the latter section of Tories
were opposed to reform of the House of Commons. The result was that it fell wholly to
the Whigs to force it on; and the Whigs, being
weak in Parliament did not scruple to appeal
to the passions of uneducated people outside
Parliament. They encouraged "monster meetings," "monster petitions" and such like.
There were riots in favour of Reform. At

The
Whigs for
Reform of
the House
of Com-
mons,
1815-32.

one riot at Manchester in 1819 the soldiers had to be called in, and several people were shot. Very likely these were only innocent spectators and not rioters at all; those who get up riots are usually careful to keep out of the way when their suppression begins. Stiff laws were passed in Parliament to prevent such riotous meetings for the future.

From 1820–30 the question of Reform was never for a moment allowed to slumber, and at last in 1832 the Duke of Wellington, who, though opposed to Reform himself, was always moderate and sensible, advised the Tories to give way, and a "Reform Bill" was at last got through both Houses, an eminently sensible and moderate Bill. The number of members in the House was not increased, but the absurd old boroughs with few or no inhabitants lost their right of sending members, and the great growing towns got that right. All persons in the counties with a moderate amount of property got votes for election of members, and all persons in the towns who had a house worth £10 a year. The educated people of Great Britain and Ireland were very fairly represented in the House of Commons between 1832 and 1867. *The Reform Bill, 1832.*

But this did not stop agitation outside. A group of men called "Chartists" began to cry *Fresh agitation;*

The Chartists, 1832-48.

out for something more, for the representation of the uneducated as well. They demanded that every grown-up man should have a vote, that members of Parliament should be paid, that a new Parliament should be elected every year, and so on. These men tried to get up riots in favour of their demands; in 1848 it looked as if these riots were going to be serious.

Later Reform Bills, 1867-85.

But the thing fizzled out somehow. Twice since that time new Reform Bills have been passed, one by each party in the State, by the Tories in 1867 (now called "Conservatives"), and by the Whigs in 1885 (now called "Liberals" or "Radicals"). On each occasion the vote was given to poorer and less educated classes of the people, and on the latter occasion the distinction between counties and boroughs was practically abolished; every district in Britain, whether of town or country, is now represented in the House of Commons pretty nearly according to the number of people living in it.

The Irish members.

Unfortunately one exception to this principle has been allowed. With the exception of those from Ulster, the Irish members of the House of Commons since the Union of 1800 have never been loyal to our system of government, but have continually cried out for a separate Parliament in Dublin. The first

great agitator for this purpose was the orator
Daniel O'Connell, in the reigns of George IV
and William IV and at the beginning of Victoria's reign. He has been followed by many
others, notably by Mr. Parnell, and the
agitation is still continuing. In order to hush
this cry, British statesmen have allowed Ireland
to have many more members of the House
of Commons than the population of that
island warrants. More than one statesman,
especially the famous Mr. Gladstone in 1885
and 1892, has thought of conciliating the Irish,
by granting them, under the name of "Home
Rule," the separate Parliament which they
demand. But most people fear that a separate
Irish Parliament would be followed by a complete separation between Ireland and Great
Britain, by the establishment of an Irish
Republic, and by the oppression of the well-to-
do and intelligent classes of Irishmen, who are
certainly loyal to the British Crown. All
British politicians, on both sides, have, during
the last seventy years, made haste to remove
every real, and, indeed, every imaginary
grievance of the Irish people, though they have
earned no gratitude by doing so.

As regards the Ministers of the Crown, The
whom we may consider next after Parliament Ministers
as an "institution" of the country, it has been of the
Crown.

well understood, ever since George III's death, that the King "reigns but does not govern." He takes as his ministers men who are agreeable to the majority in the existing House of Commons. In quiet times there is a new House of Commons about every five or six years and there must be one every seven years. There is, therefore, very likely to be a change of ministry every time there is a new House. Before the first Reform Bill there were only about 300,000 electors; there are now over 7,000,000. But, oddly enough, the larger the number of electors, the more frequent are the changes of public opinion. In former days Whigs or Tories might well hold office through three or four successive parliaments; now it is very rare that either party holds it through two. The opinion of the electors has a curious habit of swinging right round in a very short space of time; and, so, great changes in our rulers are of frequent occurrence.

The Cabinet.   These rulers or ministers we call the "Cabinet"; and in the Cabinet you will always find a "Prime Minister," generally called the "First Lord of the Treasury," at the head of the whole thing; it is with him that the real responsibility lies. He explains to the King what he and his friends think ought to be done; and, when he is a wise man, he generally finds that the King's advice on the matter is very well worth listening to. If the King does not approve of what his Prime Minister suggests he can always dismiss him; but it is of no use his doing this unless he can appoint some one else whom the existing House of Commons will follow; or unless he is prepared to dismiss the existing House of Commons and call a new Parliament. The King will do this last if he feels sure that the Minister and the existing House are leading the nation astray or are leading it where it doesn't want to go. Any very "revolutionary" proposal, such as the abolition of either House of Parliament, the surrender of India or the Colonies, the reduction of the Navy very far below the strength necessary to defend the Empire, might quite conceivably obtain for a moment a majority in the House of Commons, and, though it is unlikely, it is just possible that the House of Lords might be terrified into accepting it. But *then* it would be the duty of the King to interfere, and to dismiss, at all costs, the Ministry which was rash enough to make such a proposal.

Besides the Prime Minister, the most important members of the Cabinet are the Chancellor of the Exchequer, who manages money matters, the Secretaries of State for War, for

Foreign Affairs, for the Colonies, for Home
Affairs, and the First Lord of the Admiralty,
who manages the Navy. Each is responsible
for some particular part of the task of government; but all must agree upon all important
questions, and the minister who doesn't agree
with the rest of the Cabinet must resign.

The most distinguished Prime Ministers since 1815. I shall not trouble you with a list of the
ministries that have held office since 1815;
two things only you should remember: first,
that ministries are more short-lived now than
they used to be; and secondly, that they are
more dominated by the Prime Minister for
the time being than they used to be. The most
distinguished Prime Ministers have been Mr.
Canning (died 1827), Lord Grey (died 1845),
Sir Robert Peel (died 1850), Lord Palmerston
(died 1865), Lord Beaconsfield, better known
as Mr. Disraeli (died 1881), Mr. Gladstone
(died 1898), and Lord Salisbury (died 1903).
Each in his own way has contributed something to the greatness of England; but each,
with the exception of Sir Robert Peel, has had
a weak side. Speaking generally, those ministers who have paid most attention to finances
and to internal reform have been less successful in upholding the honour of England
abroad and in strengthening the Army and
Navy.

With regard to the law and the law courts, The Law Courts. it is not such a very different England in which we live from what it was in the days of our great-grandfathers. The House of Lords is still the highest "Court of Appeal" in Great Britain and Ireland; but to hear appeals, only those peers sit who are specially appointed to be judges for that purpose. There is a Court of Appeal below it and a High Court of Justice below that. The judges are still appointed by the King, and still "go on circuit" four times a year to the several districts of England to try criminal cases, as they have done since the fourteenth century. There are also small courts called "county courts," for small lawsuits, in some sixty different districts in England. Scotland has kept, since the Union of 1708, her own system of law and law courts The Scottish Law Courts. entirely different from ours, but from them also you can appeal to the House of Lords. Ireland has the same system of law as ours, but has her own law courts with appeal to the House of Lords. Each colony in the Empire has its own law courts and judges, and appeals from them and from the Indian law courts come not to the House of Lords, but to a few great judges in the Privy Council. Reform of the Criminal Law, 1818-50.

The one really great law reform has been that of the criminal law. In 1815 over one

hundred and sixty crimes were still supposed
to be punished with death.   There are now only
two, high treason and wilful murder, and, unfortunately, people who commit high treason
are now too often let off. In 1815 a thief
might be hanged if he stole five shillings'
worth of goods from a shop! He hardly ever
was hanged, because he was tried by a jury and
a judge, and juries preferred to declare him
"not guilty" rather than allow him to be
hanged; so, as a rule, he got off altogether.
Even of those who were convicted and condemned to be hanged not one tenth were
hanged.   And this was because public opinion
was more merciful than the law. From 1788
onward criminals who had just escaped hanging used to be "transported" to Australia,
and this went on till 1840. The other settlers
in that continent naturally objected very much
to this; and we now send our criminals to
"penal servitude" in large prisons at Dart-
moor and Portland instead. No words can
be too hard to use against the Tory ministers
like Lord Eldon, who, year after year, from
1815 to 1830, obstructed the reform of the
criminal laws as much as they could; most
of the reforms in them were due to the
Whigs or to the more enlightened Tory, Sir
Robert Peel.

To Tory Governments belongs the credit of beginning to remove the laws which made a man's admission to Parliament depend upon his religious opinions. Both Lord Castlereagh, who died in 1822, and Mr. Canning, who died in 1827, had always been anxious to admit Catholics to Parliament; but it was just after Canning's death that, first the Protestant Dissenters in 1828, and then the Catholics in 1829, were admitted. Jews had to wait till 1853, and those who openly declared their disbelief in any religion at all till 1884. The support of the State to the Protestant Church in Ireland, which dated from the time of Elizabeth, was taken away in 1868. The zeal of the Church of England was, from 1829 onward, quickened by men like Newman and Dr. Pusey, and religion is now a far more vital force in our daily lives than it was at the end of George III's reign. Differences of opinion upon religion still exist, and still occasionally lead to squabbles between Churchmen and Dissenters, but they are being smoothed away; of all passions, religious hatred is now seen to be the most odious, and all reasonable men acknowledge that the teaching of sound morality is the main duty of all religious bodies. Without religion there can be no good morals, and without good morals the wisest laws are futile.

Admission of Dissenters, Catholics, and Jews to Parliament, 1828-53.

Church revival, 1829.

Other
reforms.

The Whigs are responsible for the abolition of slavery in our West Indian Islands (1833); the importation of slaves from Africa thither had been prohibited as far back as 1807. They

The New
Poor Law,
1834.

can also claim the credit of the "New Poor Law" (1834), which refused to give food or money to the idle and improvident unless they would come into the "workhouse"; and this law made workhouse life sufficiently unpleasant, so that lots of idle loafers, who had hitherto "lived on the rates," preferred to earn their

Munici-
pal re-
form,
1835.

own living. The same Whig Government in 1835 reformed the town councils of our cities and boroughs in such a way that every householder now gets a vote for the election of his town council. In 1889 a Conservative government extended this plan to the country dis-

County
Councils,
1889.

tricts also, and in each shire a "county council" is now elected, which manages all local business such as the keeping up of roads, bridges, lunatic asylums, and the police. It was Sir Robert Peel who created the present magnificent force of policemen, and its members are still sometimes, in sport, called after him "bobbies" and "peelers."

National
Educa-
tion, 1870.

Perhaps the most important of all reforms of the nineteenth century was the introduction in 1870 for all classes of the people of a system of schools, supported by the State and paid

for by a rate on each district. Every one is
now compelled to attend some kind of school,
and a man may be sent to prison if he refuses
to send his children to school. When I was
a boy it was quite common to meet people
who could neither read nor write; now it is
the rarest thing in the world.

There was one burning question all through
the first thirty years of this period, of which
I have yet told you nothing; and it was the
most serious of all — the question of food.
Great Britain and Ireland could no longer
grow enough corn to feed their great and rapidly
increasing populations. For the two and
twenty years which ended in 1815, governments had been too busy saving the very
existence of Britain and of Europe to pay
attention to this question. But now followed
a period of peace, in which both the bill for
the war had to be paid, and this terrible food
question faced in earnest.

The bill for the war was an enormous one;
in 1793 the National Debt was not much over
200 millions; in 1815 it was over 900 millions;
the interest to be paid on it annually had gone
up from 8 to 33 millions. Taxation had been
enormously heavy, and every one cried out
for its reduction. To this cry for a reduction
of taxes the government was perhaps right

The food question.

The National Debt, from 1815.

to turn a deaf ear as long as that frightful bill remained unpaid; and, also, during these ninety-five years, very little of that bill has really been paid off; the debt is still over 700 millions, though the interest annually paid on each £100 of it has been reduced to £2 10*s.* 0*d.*

But there can be no excuse for the deaf ear which the government turned to the question of food. The price of corn still varied with each harvest, and varied enormously. But now it was beginning to be possible to import corn from America, from Russia, and from several other places. And the proper thing to do would have been to put a moderate customs duty on the importation of corn, a duty which should vary with the price of corn in the London market. Instead of doing this, Parliament in 1815 passed a law saying that no corn should be imported at all until the price in London was 80*s.* a quarter, which meant that a loaf of bread would cost about 9*d.* This was called "protecting" the British farmers and the British landowners, who of course could get high prices and high rents when the price of corn was high; but it came very near to mean starving the British labourer. Those who upheld this plan were called "Protectionists"; those who wished to admit cheap foreign corn were called "Free Traders."

The "Corn Laws" became the subject of Agitation against them. an agitation far fiercer than that for Reform of Parliament, and with much more reason. Over and over again there was danger of a rising of the poor labourers against all who owned or farmed land. Even when there was not a bad harvest, and when the price of corn was far below the 80*s.* a quarter, it was easy for agitators to persuade the poor that they *must* be very badly off; and, especially in the days before the Reform Bill, the outcry of the poor against the rich was a most distressing feature of the age. You cannot expect much reason from people who are really hard up for food, or who expect to be hard up for food in a few months. At last, in 1845, there appeared the most manifest symptoms of a coming famine in Ireland, owing to the failure of the potato crop. Sir Robert Peel, Their repeal, 1846. who was then in power, and who had hitherto been a moderate "Protectionist," turned right round, and in 1846 abolished the Corn Laws altogether. He was too late to save Ireland from famine, which came in all its horrors in 1847, and, by death or emigration to America, reduced the Irish people by more than a third of their numbers. But he believed that he had saved any portion of our islands from the chance of such a disaster for the future.

Decay of of agriculture.

For a long time after the abolition of the Corn Laws it still paid the farmers to grow corn in Britain. But as the empty lands of America and Canada came to be more and more peopled and cultivated, and when the introduction of steamships brought down the cost and shortened the time needed to bring corn across the Atlantic, it began to pay them less and less. And now we buy not only almost all our corn, but most of our meat, and a good deal of our wool, fruit and butter, from abroad also. The sad result has been that the land of England is rapidly going out of cultivation, and that our villages are being deserted in favour of our towns, where we cannot expect so strong and healthy a race to grow up as that of our grandfathers who lived by work in the open fields.

Imported food.

There is, moreover, a most serious danger behind. If England should ever be defeated in a great war at sea, it would be impossible for us to get our food at all, and our population would simply starve. Therefore, at whatever cost to ourselves, it is our duty to keep our Navy so strong that it must be forever impossible for us to be defeated at sea.

Big Steamers.

"Oh, where are you going to, all you Big
    Steamers,
  With England's own coal, up and down the
    salt seas?"
"We are going to fetch you your bread and
    your butter,
  Your beef, pork, and mutton, eggs, apples,
    and cheese."

"And where will you fetch it from, all you
    Big Steamers,
  And where shall I write you when you are
    away?"
"We fetch it from Melbourne, Quebec, and
    Vancouver,
  Address us at Hobart, Hong-kong, and
    Bombay."

"But if anything happened to all you Big
    Steamers,
  And suppose you were wrecked up and down
    the salt sea?"
"Why, you'd have no coffee or bacon for
    breakfast,
  And you'd have no muffins or toast for your
    tea."

"Then I'll pray for fine weather for all you
    Big Steamers,
  For little blue billows and breezes so soft."
"Oh, billows and breezes don't bother Big
    Steamers,
  For we're iron below and steel-rigging aloft."

"Then I'll build a new lighthouse for all you
        Big Steamers.
    With plenty wise pilots to pilot you through,"
"Oh the Channel's as bright as a ball room
        already,
    And pilots are thicker than pilchards at
        Looe."

"Then what can I do for you, all you Big
        Steamers,
    Oh, what can I do for your comfort and good?"
"Send out your big warships to watch your
        big waters,
    That no one may stop us from bringing you
        food.

*"For the bread that you eat and the biscuit you
        nibble,*
    *The sweets that you suck and the joints that
        you carve,*
*They are brought to you daily by all us Big
        Steamers,*
    *And if any one hinders our coming you'll
        starve!"*

Free
trade.   The principle of "free trade" has been carried into all departments of life. When Sir
Robert Peel took office in 1841 there were
over twelve hundred articles on which duty
had to be paid when they were imported from
abroad. There are now only sixteen such
articles, and the only ones of any importance
are wine, spirits and tobacco (all of which are

"luxuries," as opposed to "necessaries" of life). When this policy was first adopted it was expected that all other nations would soon adopt "free trade" also, but they have not done so; and we have even allowed our own colonies to put on customs duties against the importation of British goods to their ports. Proposals are now on foot, and are maintained by a large party in Britain, to go back upon this principle of "free trade," and to impose a moderate "tariff" on the importation of goods from all nations which will not admit British goods to their ports without a duty. It is not my business to express an opinion as to whether this would be wise or not. No doubt "free trade all round" would be the most splendid thing in the world for all nations if all would agree to carry it out.

The next point to which I must direct your attention is the growth of the British Empire. Soon after Victoria became Queen a cry for "self-government" began to be heard from the colonies. There were five and forty British colonies all told, and the joke went round that they were governed by three and twenty clerks of the "Colonial Office" in Downing Street, London. This was not quite true, as most of our colonies had little councils of their own, which in some cases were even

Growth of the Empire.

Cry of
colonies
for self-
govern-
ment;
Canada,
1839.

elected. It was in Canada that the cry for
a more free system first arose. Many of the
inhabitants of its two provinces were of old
French descent, and spoke, as they still speak,
French. There were mutterings of rebellion
out there, and threats that the Canadians
would join the United States of America.
In order to prevent this and to satisfy the Canadians, the experiment was tried in 1840 of
giving them the beginnings of a regular Parliament like our own, with a ministry responsible to that Parliament and named by a
Governor representing the Crown.

The gradual extension of the Dominion of
Canada to include the territories known as
Ontario and British Columbia right up to the
Island of Vancouver was the work of the
middle period of Victoria's reign; and during
the same period the United States of America
were extending westward and ever more
westward till they reached the Pacific Ocean.
In "British North America," Newfoundland
now alone remains a colony separated from
the "Dominion of Canada" and with a Parliament of its own.

The
Austra-
lian
colonies,
1787-
1910.

The first of the Australian colonies in point
of time was New South Wales, to which, as
I told you, our criminals continued to be sent
from 1788 till 1840; West Australia dates from

1829, South Australia and Victoria from 1836, and Queensland from 1850. These all soon began to cry out for parliamentary governments of their own; and in 1850 a Whig ministry began to give it to them freely. Quite in our own days an Act of the British Parliament has made all the Australian colonies into a single "Federation" of States, with a "federal" or united Parliament for the whole continent. New Zealand, which was first recognized as a colony in 1840, has got her own Parliament and is not included in this Federation. The great wealth of both New Zealand and Australia consists in their vast flocks of sheep; these colonies are to the British manufacturers of woollen goods what England was to the Flemish weavers in the fourteenth century, namely, the source of the "raw material" of their industry. There are also great gold mines in Australia.

The Australian Federation

Next in order of importance of our colonies comes South Africa with its wonderful climate. Its great importance to us, when we took it from the Dutch in the Great War, was as a station on the road to India; but, since the opening of the Suez Canal in 1869, we have now got a shorter road thither.

South Africa, 1806-1910.

In Canada we had really little difficulty in making good friends with our new French subjects, for they hated and feared the pushing Americans, whose territory lay to the south, and they knew that we would defend them against these men. In Australia we had nothing but a few miserable blacks, who could hardly use even bows and arrows in fight. In New Zealand we had a more warlike branch of the same race, called the Maoris, to deal with. But in South Africa we had not only really fierce savages like Zulus and Kaffirs, but also a large population of Dutch farmers and traders, who had been settled there since the middle of the seventeenth century.

The Dutch Boers. These were called the "Boers"; they thoroughly disliked our rule, and they were continually retiring further and further from Cape Town into the interior of the Continent. They treated the native Kaffirs very badly, and objected when we tried to protect these against them. Besides "Cape Colony" (at the Cape of Good Hope itself), there were Dutch or half-Dutch States at Natal, on the Orange River, and beyond the Vaal River. One by one, in the reign of Victoria, each of these was annexed by Great Britain, and the last years of our great Queen were made sorrowful by the war which we had to fight against these brave, dogged and cunning Dutch farmers of the Transvaal. This war, though

against a mere handful of men, strained the
resources of Great Britain to the utmost; it
showed us how very badly equipped we were
for war upon any serious scale; but it also led
to a great outburst of patriotism all over the
Empire, and our other colonies sent hundreds
of their best young men to help us. In the
end we won, and peace was signed in 1902; a
"Federation" of all the South African colonies
with a central Parliament at Cape Town has
recently been concluded, and the hatred between British and Dutch is now almost a thing
of the past. South Africa owes its recent prosperity more to the discovery of great gold
and diamond mines than to agriculture; but
almost anything can be grown there.

The South African Federation

The vast territory of Rhodesia, in the centre
of the dark continent of Africa, and the British
"Protectorates" of Uganda, British East
Africa, and British Central Africa further to
the north, are still, as yet, more or less unde-
veloped; but great things may be expected of
all of them, both as agricultural, commercial
and mining colonies. The natives everywhere
welcome the mercy and justice of our rule,
and they are no longer liable, as they were
before we came, to be carried off as slaves by
Arab slave dealers.

Other African colonies.

There are other countries, like Ceylon, the

The West Indies, etc.

West Indies, the several stations on the north-west African coast, Singapore on the Straits of Malacca, Guiana on the north coast of South America, and islands too numerous to mention, both in the Pacific and Atlantic Oceans, which belong to Great Britain. But most of these are called "Crown Colonies" and do not enjoy any form of Parliamentary government nor need it. The prosperity of the West Indies, once our richest possession, has very largely declined since slavery was abolished in 1833. The population is mainly black, descended from slaves imported in previous centuries, or of mixed black and white race; lazy, vicious and incapable of any serious improvement, or of work except under compulsion. In such a climate a few bananas will sustain the life of a negro quite sufficiently; why should he work to get more than this? He is quite happy and quite useless, and spends any extra wages which he may earn upon finery.

Future of the Empire. What the future of our self-governing and really great colonies may be it is hard to say. Perhaps the best thing that could happen would be a "Federation" of the whole British Empire, with a central Parliament in which all the colonies should get representatives, with perfect free trade between the whole, and with an

imperial army and navy to which all should
contribute payments. But where and when
shall we find the statesman great and bold
enough to propose it?

Our Indian Empire must be treated to a
few lines by itself. It is not a colony but a
"Dependency of the Crown." The extension
of our rule over the whole Indian peninsula
was made possible, first by the exclusion of
any other European Power (when we had
once beaten off the French there), and secondly
by the fact that the weaker states and princes
continually called in our help against the stronger.
From our three starting-points of Calcutta,
Madras and Bombay, we have gradually
swallowed the whole country; though some
states keep their native princes, these are all
sworn subjects of King George as "Emperor
of India," just as in feudal times a great feudal
Earl was a sworn subject of his King. Our rule
has been infinitely to the good of all the three
hundred millions of the different races who
inhabit that richly peopled land.

Until 1858 the old "East India Company,"
founded at the end of Elizabeth's reign, was
the nominal sovereign. Its early conquests
had been made over the unwarlike races of
Bengal and of the South; next, in the reign
of George III, over the gallant robbers who

Our Indian Empire;

its growth till 1910.

swarmed over the central plains and were
called Mahrattas. Early in Victoria's time
we had to meet those magnificent fighters the
Sikhs of the Punjaub, and the fierce Afghans
of the north-western mountains. Both gave
us from time to time terrible lessons; but
British patience and courage triumphed over
all. As we conquered them, so we enrolled in
our Indian army all the best fighting men of
these various races; of that army the Sikhs
are now the backbone; but the Afghans have
still to be kept at bay beyond the northern
mountains. They are the "tigers from the
North"; and, if our rule were for a moment
taken away, they would ˙sweep down and
slay and enslave all the defenceless dwellers on
the plains.

The
Indian
Mutiny,
1857.

In 1857 our carelessness and mismanagement
of this vast Empire, together with the religious
fear inspired among the Indians by the introduction of European inventions such as steam
and railways, brought about the most serious
danger that ever threatened British India, a
mutiny in our Indian army. The instigator
of the revolt was a man who claimed to be the
representative of the old Mahratta rulers; the
rebels took Delhi, the oldest capital city of
India, and set up a shadow of an Emperor.
They perpetrated terrible cruelties upon defence-

less Englishwomen and children. But Southern India remained perfectly loyal and quiet; so did several of the old native princes; while the gallant Sikhs and the Ghoorkas of Nepaul came to our help in crowds. British troops were poured in as fast as possible, though in those days that was not very fast. The siege of Delhi and the relief of Lucknow were the greatest feats that were performed; and the names of John Lawrence, John Nicholson, Colin Campbell and Henry Havelock became forever immortal. When the mutiny was finally put down in 1858 the Crown took over the sovereignty from the East India Company, which ceased to exist; and, twenty years later, Queen Victoria was proclaimed "Empress of India."

Another "Eastern" state, much nearer home, came to us in 1882, Egypt. It was sorely against the will of our statesmen that it came. Egypt had, till 1840, been a province of the Turkish Empire, and had since that date been most shockingly misgoverned by a series of Mahommedan rulers, called Khedives. When, in 1869, the canal was cut by French engineers through the Isthmus of Suez, which separates the Red Sea from the Mediterranean, and when a new route to India for the largest vessels was thus opened, it became of the first

Egypt, 1882-1910.

importance to us to keep this route safe and
open. France at first shared with us the
"Protectorate" of Egypt which was then
rendered necessary; but, when an insurrection
of natives broke out in 1882, the task of suppressing it fell to us alone, and, when it was
over, the sole Protectorate of Egypt became
ours also. These were comparatively easy
tasks, for the native Egyptian was not a good
fighting man; but, as in India there is always
a "tiger from the North" to be feared, so in
Egypt there was always a "lion from the
South." By this "lion" I mean the fierce
tribes of the desert which is called the "Soudan," and of the Upper Nile Valley; they are
Mohammedans by faith and of mixed Arab
and negro race. These wild men were always
ready to spring upon the fertile valley of
the Lower Nile. Our Ministers at home
too often turned a blind eye to these dangers,
and their blindness cost us the life of the
gallant general, Charles Gordon. It was
not till 1898 that these "Soudanese" were
finally subdued; and the Soudan is now
governed by us as a dependency of Egypt.
The justice and mercy which these countries
had not known since the fall of the Roman
Empire is now in full measure given to them
by the British.

This great expansion of the British Empire
during the last ninety-five years has not come
about without a great deal of jealousy from
the other European powers; and this jealousy
was never more real or more dangerous than it
is to-day. But the one European war which
we have fought since 1815 had nothing to do
with the expansion of our Empire. Jealousy of other European States.

The other nations have realized that this
Empire was founded on trade, that it has to
be maintained by a navy, and that it has
resulted in good government of the races subject to us. So, though they have envied us
and given us ugly names, they have, on the
whole, paid us the compliment by trying to
copy us, to build up their navies, to increase
their manufactures, to plant colonies and to govern subject races well. Some people think that
they have not succeeded in this last object so
well as ourselves. But all European nations
are now keenly interested in trade rivalry;
whether this will end peaceably or not remains still to be seen. Trade rivalry.

All civilized nations, except ourselves and
the Americans, have also set themselves to
arm and drill all their citizens, so as to fit themselves for war on a gigantic scale at any moment.
If ever a great war breaks out in Europe, the
nation that is most ready with its fleet and its Necessity for defence of the Empire.

army will win; in the greatest war of the nineteenth century (that of 1870 between France
and Germany) it needed only a telegram of
two words to put the German army in motion
in a few hours. On the other hand, all the
great mechanical inventions of recent years,
railways, telegraphs, enormous guns, iron
ships, airships, have made war, not only much
more terrible, but infinitely more expensive;
and, so, each nation will naturally shrink from
being the first to start a war, for defeat will
spell absolute and irretrievable ruin. But I
don't think there can be any doubt that the
only safe thing for all of us who love our country
is to learn soldiering at once, and to be prepared to fight at any moment.

The
Crimean
War,
1854-6.

The one European war which we fought in
the nineteenth century was the "Crimean
War." England and France fought Russia,
on behalf of Turkey, in 1854-6. The Turkish
State was believed to be crumbling, and
certainly the Turks were real barbarians, who
governed their provinces very badly; and,
being Mohammedans, they denied all justice
to their Christian subjects. Russia claimed
to protect these subjects, but every one knew
that she only did this in order to swallow as
much of the Turkish Empire as she could.
All other powers dreaded Russia, a half bar-

barous state of vast size, and full of very brave, if very stupid, soldiers. Some people think that the cunning Frenchmen led England by the nose into this war, and that it was no business of ours. It was fought in the peninsula of the Crimea, on the northern coast of the Black Sea. There were some terrible battles, those of the Alma, of Balaclava, of Inkermann, in the autumn of 1854; then the war settled into a long siege of Sebastopol, during an awful winter, in which the sufferings of our army in the trenches before the city were terrible. In the end Russia had to own herself beaten, and Turkey, whom people called the "Sick Man of Europe," was propped up again. Though many of his other provinces have revolted from him, he is still alive, and now even in a fair way to recover his health, and to govern more decently than before.

One point I have left till the last. When your great-grandfathers were young, the fastest method of travelling was in a stage-coach with four horses at ten miles an hour, or in a private (and very expensive) post-chaise which might perhaps do twelve miles an hour. When they wanted to light their candles (and they had nothing else to light) they had to strike a spark with a bit of steel on a bit of flint. The navy was built of oak instead of

Changes in English life, 1815-1910; the age of inventions.

steel, and moved by sails instead of steam. Letters cost two pence apiece for the smallest weight and the smallest distance; a single sheet letter from London to Edinburgh cost 1s. 1d.

Look round you and see in what a different England you now live. Gas was first used in the streets of London in 1812; but gas already is going, and electric light is taking its place. The first railway was opened in 1829 between Liverpool and Manchester; already people are wondering when the first service of passenger airships will begin to cut out railways for long journeys, as electric tramways and motor cars have begun to cut out horses and railways alike for short ones. The first steamship began to ply on the Clyde in 1812; it was of three horse-power and moved at five miles an hour; the *Mauretania*, of 30,000 horse-power, now crosses the Atlantic in less than five days. During the Great War a system of wooden signals from hill top to hill top, worked by hand, would carry a message from Dover to London in about an hour; now the electric telegraph flashes messages round the world in a few minutes. By another kind of wire, the telephone, a man in London can talk to a man in Paris, and they can hear each other's voices and laughter. The discovery of chloroform in 1847 has reduced human suffering to a degree which we can hardly conceive; and the other improvements in medicine and surgery have saved and prolonged countless useful, as well as many useless, lives.

THE SECRET OF THE MACHINES.

We were taken from the ore-bed and the mine,
  We were melted in the furnace and the pit —
We were cast and wrought and hammered
    to design,
  We were cut and filed and tooled and gauged
    to fit.
Some water, coal, and oil is all we ask,
  And a thousandth of an inch to give us play,
And now if you will set us to our task,
  We will serve you four and twenty hours
    a day!

  We can pull and haul and push and lift
    and drive,
  We can print and plough and weave and
    heat and light,
  We can run and jump and swim and fly
    and dive,
  We can see and hear and count and read
    and write!

Wireless
Tele-
graphs.

Would you call a friend from half across the
world?
If you'll let us have his name and town
and state,
You shall see and hear your crackling question hurled
Across the arch of heaven while you wait.

Marine
Engines.

Has he answered? Does he need you at his
side?
You can start this very evening if you choose,
And take the Western Ocean in the stride
Of thirty thousand horses and some screws!

The boat-express is waiting your command!
You will find the *Mauretania* at the quay,
Till her captain turns the lever 'neath
his hand,
And the monstrous nine-decked city goes
to sea.

Loco-
motives,
Pumps
and Min-
ing Tools.

Do you wish to make the mountains bare
their head
And lay their new-cut forests at your feet?
Do you want to turn a river in its bed,
And plant a barren wilderness with wheat?
Shall we pipe aloft and bring you water down
From the never-failing cisterns of the snows,
To work the mills and tramways in your town,
And irrigate your orchards as it flows?

It is easy! Give us dynamite and drills!
Watch the iron-shouldered rocks lie down
    and quake
As the thirsty desert-level floods and fills,
And the valley we have dammed becomes
    a lake!

But remember, please, the Law by which *All To-*
  we live, *gether.*
  We are not built to comprehend a lie,
We can neither love nor pity nor forgive,
  If you make a slip in handling us you die!
We are greater than the Peoples or the Kings —
  Be humble, as you crawl beneath our rods!—
Our touch can alter all created things,
  We are everything on earth — except The
    Gods!

Though our smoke may hide the Heavens
    from your eyes,
It will vanish and the stars will shine again,
Because for all our power and weight and size,
We are nothing more than children of your
    brain!

In the common sense of the word "happy," *What is*
these and a thousand other inventions have no *the lesson of history?*
doubt made us happier than our great-grand-
fathers were. Have they made us better,

braver, more self-denying, more manly men and boys; more tender, more affectionate, more home-loving women and girls? It is for you boys and girls, who are growing up, to resolve that you will be all these things, and to be true to your resolutions.

The Glory of the Garden.

Our England is a garden that is full of stately
    views,
Of borders, beds and shrubberies and lawns
    and avenues,
With statues on the terraces and peacocks
    strutting by;
But the Glory of the Garden lies in more than
    meets the eye.

For where the old thick laurels grow, along the
    thin red wall,
You'll find the tool and potting-sheds which
    are the heart of all.
The cold-frames and the hot-houses, the dung-
    pits and the tanks,
The rollers, carts and drain-pipes, with the
    barrows and the planks.

And there you'll see the gardeners, the men and
    'prentice boys
Told off to do as they are bid and do it without
    noise;

For, except when seeds are planted and we shout
    to scare the birds,
The Glory of the Garden it abideth not in
    words.

And some can pot begonias and some can bud
    a rose,
And some are hardly fit to trust with anything
    that grows;
But they can roll and trim the lawns and sift
    the sand and loam,
For the Glory of the Garden occupieth all
    who come.

Our England is a garden, and such gardens
    are not made
By singing, "Oh, how beautiful," and sitting
    in the shade,
While better men than we go out and start
    their working lives
At grubbing weeds from gravel-paths with
    broken dinner-knives.

There's not a pair of legs so thin, there's not
    a head so thick,
There's not a hand so weak and white, nor yet
    a heart so sick,
But it can find some needful job that's crying
    to be done,
For the Glory of the Garden glorifieth every one.

Then seek your job with thankfulness and
    work till further orders,
If it's only netting strawberries or killing
    slugs on borders;
And when your back stops aching and your
    hands begin to harden,
You will find yourself a partner in the Glory
    of the Garden.

Oh, Adam was a gardener, and God who made
    him sees
That half a proper gardener's work is done
    upon his knees,
So when your work is finished, you can wash
    your hands and pray
For the Glory of the Garden that it may not
    pass away!
And the Glory of the Garden it shall never pass
    away!